THE HUDSUCKER P

Also by Joel and Ethan Coen

BARTON FINK and MILLER'S CROSSING

THE
HUDSUCKER PROXY

Ethan and Joel Coen
and Sam Raimi

faber and faber
LONDON · BOSTON

First published in 1994
by Faber and Faber Limited
3 Queen Square London WC1N 3AU

Photoset in Plantin by Parker Typesetting Service, Leicester
Printed in England by Clays Ltd, St Ives plc

Photographs from *The Hudsucker Proxy* by
Jim Bridges, © Warner Bros
Photograph of the Coen Brothers © the Douglas Brothers

A CIP record for this book is available
from the British Library

ISBN 0-571-17190-7

2 4 6 8 10 9 7 5 3 1

CONTENTS

The Coen brothers, Joel and Ethan (photo by the Douglas brothers).

INTRODUCTION
A Conversation with Joel Silver

The following conversation between Dennis Jacobson, professor of cinema studies at the University of Iowa, and producer Joel Silver, is reprinted with the permission of *Cine Quarterly*, where it first appeared in the autumn of 1993.

DJ: First of all, congratulations on *The Hudsucker Proxy*.

JS: Thank you, thanks very much.

DJ: The first question – the obvious question – is, Joel Silver and the Coen brothers – it seems an odd marriage. How did it work out? What was it like working with them? Any friction, or –

JS: No no, it was easy. It was great. I have such respect for these guys – it was tremendous. I mean, to be quite frank they would whine occasionally, but it was generally a very easy relationship.

DJ: When would they whine?

JS: Just the occasional, you know, when they couldn't get their way. They would kvetch about – say, when I suggested they use Paul Newman. 'No, he's too big, he's iconic – he represents a larger – ' a whole line of bullshit. I'm just saying it could degenerate sometimes into whining.

DJ: So they did not control the casting of the movie?

JS: Their attitude, it was funny. Like it's a sin to use a movie star. God forbid somebody should actually be enticed into the theater to see one of their movies. 'No, he's too iconic.' And Tim Robbins, that whole thing – forget about it.

DJ: Tim Robbins was not their choice either? And yet he's very good.

JS: This – I found this unbelievable at the time, but this – Ethan wanted to play the part.

DJ: Ethan Coen wanted to play the lead in the movie?

JS: Yeah. He says only he understands the character fully. He's gotta do it. He's the only one who *can* do it. It was absurd, but I let him test.

DJ: He shot, he did a screen test?

JS: Yeah. He did the scene out on the terrace where they talk about reincarnation. Some drama-coach friend of his did the girl.

DJ: How was it?

JS: What do you think how was it? It was goddamned embarrassing. It's – it was like the early days of talkies. Ethan is lumbering around on this pathetic little set they've mocked up, with his flat Midwestern voice, chopping the air with his hands, these stiff gestures, I mean, Richard Nixon doing a love scene. Stiffo. Embarrassing. So I try to tell him –

DJ: Was he –

JS: – and he wants to screen it for Warners. I said look, Ethan, this will not do you credit with the studio, and he says, Let Warners decide! Let Warners decide! I couldn't talk him out of it. So I screen it for Terry Semel and Bob Daly [Warner Brothers president and chairman], and it's over and the lights go up and no one knows where to look. Not that – see, I never told Bob and Terry it was Ethan, didn't want them to kill the movie. To this day Terry Semel thinks he saw Kevin Kline testing, in make-up. And believe me, Kevin Kline will not be offered any more Warners pictures. So anyway I tell Ethan, *mazel tov*, you almost killed the picture. And he's screaming, No, no, they just don't see it yet, they don't see it yet! Let me talk to Terry! Well, I managed to head it off.

DJ: What was Joel Coen's position on all this?

JS: Didn't know about it.

DJ: Didn't know – ?

JS: Didn't know about the test. He was – I guess he was vaguely aware that Ethan wanted to play the part, but he didn't much care. Didn't care who played it. I suggested Tim Robbins and he said fine. I don't think he ever really thought much about it.

DJ: Yet it's the –

JS: Ethan, though – he sulked, and things were never right between him and Tim. He never made his peace with it. They'd be shooting a scene and you'd see Ethan off in the corner, mouthing the lines as Tim spoke. It was pathetic.

DJ: Did he –

JS: You ask him today, he'll still tell you he should've played the part.

DJ: So Joel was not interested in the casting?

JS: The girl he was interested in. Ethan didn't give a shit about that. 'Yeah, the girl –' he'd wave his hand.

DJ: So Joel wanted Jennifer Jason Leigh?

JS: Jeanne Moreau.

DJ: Excuse me?

JS: He wanted Jeanne Moreau. He had some line of shit about how it had to be a powerful woman, a career woman, you know, an iconic strong feminine – you wouldn't believe the line of shit on this guy. He said he wanted the equivalent of Rosalind Russell. I said fuck, *get Rosalind Russell* – she's younger than Jeanne Moreau! What's Jeanne Moreau now, eighty?

DJ: And it seems so clearly an American part.

JS: Yeah, the accent! I said what, Amy Archer is French now? He says, Oh, the accent will only add to the richness of the tapestry. These guys are so full of shit. This iconic thing, which supposedly is so terrible in Paul Newman, is a great thing all of a sudden with Jeanne Moreau. And Jennifer Jason Leigh, who's coming off a very hot movie – *Single White Female* – she's dying to do the part. Young, sexy, American, and dying to do the part.

DJ: But neither of the Coens wanted –

JS: Neither of them wanted Jennifer, no. Well Ethan, you couldn't even talk to him at this point, he's just sulking about the Tim Robbins thing. And Joel didn't know who Jennifer was. So I screen some of her movies for him. And he's not even really watching. 'What about Moreau?' So I tell him – it's bullshit, but I tell him we tried to make a deal with Moreau but she isn't interested. She turned us down. And this kind of takes the starch out of Joel. 'What about a creative meeting?' 'No no, she's passed.' So okay, so Jennifer, fine. But now *he's* moping for the rest of the picture.

DJ: So you're saying, their dream cast –

JS: Joel and Ethan's dream cast was Ethan as Norville, Jeanne Moreau as the girl, and Joe Blow as the bad guy. *You* could've done the bad guy. They would've been thrilled.

DJ: Uh-huh.

JS: So they don't get their cast, and believe me they're not gracious about it. Whiners. On the set they just sort of retreat into their storyboards. Don't talk to the actors. Just play with their little storyboards. Joel looks through the camera, looks at the storyboards, walks in and shoves Paul Newman a couple of steps to the left. Just shoves. This is Butch Cassidy here! This man is iconic! You don't shove!

DJ: How did the actors respond?

JS: Oh, actors.

DJ: So now, was the atmosphere, was it –

JS: Well I kind of sorted things out. I was sort of the *tummler*. I kept things going. Always up, always ebullient. The atmosphere – it didn't bother the Coens. I mean, in their minds it was never a comedy anyway.

DJ: Never a comedy?!

JS: No no, straight. You see that clearly in Ethan's screen test.

DJ: Would you work with them again?

JS: Yeah, sure.

DJ: Mm. I ask because they sound –

JS: Oh, I've worked with worse, believe me. This is Hollywood. I've worked with worse.

This book would not have been possible without the help of Anthony Gardner, and the kind assistance of Grace Ressler, Dawn McElwaine and Mary Murphy at Warner Bros.

The cast of *The Hudsucker Proxy* was as follows:

NORVILLE BARNES	Tim Robbins
AMY ARCHER	Jennifer Jason Leigh
SIDNEY J. MUSSBURGER	Paul Newman
WARING HUDSUCKER	Charles Durning
CHIEF	John Mahoney
BUZZ	Jim True
MOSES	Bill Cobbs
SMITTY	Bruce Campbell
ALOYSIOUS	Harry Bugin
BENNY	John Seitz
LOU	Joe Grifasi
BOARD MEMBERS	Roy Brocksmith
	I. M. Hobson
	Jerome Dempsy
	John Wylie
	Gary Allen
	Richard Woods
	John Scanlan
	Peter McPherson
DR HUGO BRONFENBRENNER	David Byrd
MAIL ROOM ORIENTER	Christopher Darga
ANCIENT SORTER	Pat Cranshaw
MAILROOM BOSS	Robert Weil
MUSSBURGER'S SECRETARY	Mary Lou Rosato
LUIGI THE TAILOR	Ernie Sarracino
MRS MUSSBURGER	Eleanor Glockner
MRS BRAITHWAITE	Kathleen Perkins
VIC TENETTA	Peter Gallagher
ZEBULON CARDOZO	Noble Willingham
THORSTENSON FINLANDSON	Thom Noble
BEATNIK BARMAN	Steve Buscemi
NEWSREEL SCIENTIST	William Duff-Griffin
ZA-ZA	Anna Nicole
DANCER	Pamela Everett

And introducing Arthur Bridges as
The Hula-Hoop Kid

Directed by	Joel Coen
Produced by	Ethan Coen
Written by	Ethan Coen, Joel Coen and Sam Raimi
Co-Producer	Graham Place
Exeutive Producers	Joel Silver, Eric Fellner and Tim Bevan
Director of Photography	Roger Deakins
Production Designer	Dennis Gassner
Costumer Designer	Richard Hornung
Music by	Carter Burwell
Edited by	Thom Noble
Supervising Sound Editor	Skip Leivsay
Casting	Donna Isaacson John Lyons
Visual Effects Produced and Supervised by	Michael J. McAlister
Mechanical Effects by	Peter Chesney Image Engineering

Blackness. A bleak wind moans.

Music cues a cut to a twinkling cityscape, seen through falling snow.

After a beat, the voice of an elderly black man:

NARRATOR

That's right . . . New York.

We are tracking high through the night sky. From the streets far below we hear the sounds of traffic and celebration, singing voices, muffled by distance and the snowfall.

. . . It's 1958 – anyway, for a few mo' minutes it is. Come midnight it's gonna be 1959. A whole 'nother feelin'. The New Year. The future . . .

We are drifting among the buildings. The tops of skyscrapers slip by left and right.

. . . Yeah, ol' Daddy Earth fixin' to start one mo' trip round the sun, an' evvybody hopin' this ride round be a little mo' giddy, a little mo' gay . . .

We are moving toward a particular skyscraper topped by a large illuminated clock.

. . . Yep . . .

We hear popping sounds.

. . . All over town champagne corks is a-poppin' . . .

A big-band waltz mixes up on the track.

. . . Over in the Waldorf the big shots is dancin' to the strains of Guy Lombardo. Down in Times Square the little folks is a-watchin' and a-waitin' fo' that big ball to drop . . .

The big-band music gives way to the chant of a distant crowd: 'Sixty! Fifty-nine! Fifty-eight!'

. . . They all tryin' to catch holt a one moment of time . . .

The chanting mixes back down to leave only the wind. Still tracking in

3

toward the top of the skyscraper, we begin to hear the hum of its enormous clock.

The clock reads one minute to twelve.

Above it, in neon, a company name: HUDSUCKER INDUSTRIES. *Below it, in neon, the company motto:* THE FUTURE IS NOW.

> . . . to be able to say – 'Right now! This is it! I *got* it!' Course by then it'll be past . . . (*More cheerfully.*) But they all happy, evvybody havin' a good time.

We are moving in on a darkened top-floor window next to the clock. The window opens.

> . . . Well, *almost* evvybody. They's a few lost souls floatin' round out there . . .

A young man crawls out of the window onto the ledge.

> . . . This one's Norville Barnes.

The man gingerly straightens up on the ledge. He is in his late twenties. He wears a leather apron. Printed on the apron: HUDSUCKER MAILROOM/The Future Is Now.

> . . . Let's move in for a closer look.

The camera obliges. We track in more quickly, ending very close.

> . . . That office he jes stepped out of is the office of the president of Hudsucker Industries. It's *his* office . . .

Norville tenses as the hum of the clock grows louder and the wind blows in his face.

> . . . How'd he get so high? An' why is he feelin' so low? Is he really gonna do it – is Norville really gonna jelly up the sidewalk?

He peers out over the ledge, preparing to make a swan dive into oblivion – but the camera's continuing move loses him from frame. We center on the enormous clock, whose mechanical hum becomes louder still.

> . . . Well, the future, that's something you can't never tell about . . .

The second hand of the clock is nearing twelve – bare seconds to midnight.

4

In sync with the clock, distant chanting from Times Square mixes up:
'Nine! Eight! Seven!'

> . . . But the past – well, that's another story . . .

OVER BLACK

The hum of the clock sinks under the hiss of an airbrake and the grinding
of gears as we cut to:

DESTINATION DISPLAY

A bus just rocking to a halt in the foreground has a front display reading
MUNCIE–NEW YORK.

A LINE OF BAGS

Being set out on the pavement. A man with the cuffs of a redcap uniform
swings one into the foreground.

It has a sticker on it, an illustration of crossed right and left hands, their
thumbs hooked and fingers spread like wings. Above the image: CLASS OF
'58. *Below the image:* MUNCIE COLLEGE OF BUSINESS
ADMINISTRATION.

After a beat a hand enters to claim the suitcase.

CITY STREET

We are following the bag as its owner bears it along. He pauses, sets it
down.

THE YOUNG MAN

Fresh-faced, eager Norville Barnes. He is gazing off at:

NIDUS EMPLOYMENT AGENCY

The sign is over a storefront window. A curtain is just being pulled open to
reveal a great job board. It is like a train station departures board, with

each of its entries flipping over occasionally to reveal a new opportunity. On offer are jobs like PASTRY CHEF, STEAMFITTER, LAY-OUT MAN, GRAVEDIGGER.

REVERSE

A small crowd has gathered, like Norville, to watch the board – men in search of jobs, of various classes and vocations, but alike in their intent gaze, their hands dug into their pockets, their hats pushed back on their heads. They bob and crane to get a better view of the chattering board. Periodically a man will leave, heading for the office, having seen a prospect he likes.

Norville stands pat, watching.

NORVILLE'S POV

An entry flips over to reveal EXECUTIVE VICE PRESIDENT.

NORVILLE

He brightens.

THE BOARD

We pan along the executive entry to the note EXPERIENCE REQUIRED.

NORVILLE

He frowns.

The crowd thins around him as men trot off to apply for their respective jobs.

We see other entries: JUNIOR EXECUTIVE. *Pan to* EXPERIENCED ONLY. EXECUTIVE MANAGER . . . MUST HAVE EXPERIENCE. BUSINESSMAN . . . EXPERIENCED.

The cross-cutting ends in a wash of superimpositions panning over Norville, who is now alone on the sidewalk: EXPERIENCED ONLY . . . EXPERIENCED . . . EXPERIENCED . . . EXPERIENCED . . .

6

ELSEWHERE: AN EXECUTIVE

Consulting notes on a clipboard, presenting some kind of report. Behind him we see only the skyline of New York City.

EXECUTIVE

– so in the third quarter we saw no signs of weakening. We're up 18 per cent over last year's third quarter gross and, needless to say, that's a new record . . .

TRACKING

Down the length of a boardroom table. Executives line either side. We are approaching the man at the far end to whom the report is being directed. He is late-middle-aged, dressed expensively but conservatively, his attention smilingly fixed on the executive who drones on:

. . . The competition continues to flag and we continue to take up the slack. Market share in most divisions is increasing, and we've opened seven new regional offices . . .

The track has ended in a close-up of the man at the end of the table, still smiling benignantly at the droning executive. The smile is serene, almost otherworldly. This man is Waring Hudsucker.

The executive at the other end of the table continues the report:

. . . Our international division has also shown vigorous upward movement in the past six months and we're looking at some exciting things in R & D . . .

The camera slowly pans off the droning executive as the big man's attention apparently wanders. We frame up on the picture window showing the skyline of New York.

. . . Sub-franchising. Don't talk to me about sub-franchising; we're making so much money in sub-franchising it isn't even funny . . .

ELSEWHERE: FOLDED-BACK WANT ADS

A pencil goes down a list of positions, ticking each one:
STREETSWEEPER – EXPERIENCED; LINOTYPE MAN –

EXPERIENCED; CANTOR (REFORM) – EXPERIENCED; SPARRING
PARTNER – EXPERIENCED.

WIDER

*Norville, sitting at a coffee shop counter, sets the pencil down. His chin is
sunk disconsolately into his palm. His hat is pushed back dejectedly on his
head. He idly stirs a cup of coffee.*

*He takes one last gulp of the coffee, then sets the cup down on the want
ads, stands, and digs into his pocket for change, turning it inside-out.*

CLOSE ON COUNTER

*Norville puts all his change on the counter. His hand hesitates; he takes a
couple of coins back. He leaves frame.*

*A waitress's hand enters from the far side of the counter. She clears away
the saucer, then the cup which has been resting on the want ads. Its
bottom leaves a perfect brown circle around one entry:*

> THE FUTURE IS NOW
> *Start building yours at*
> *Hudsucker Industries.*
> *Low pay. Long Hours.*
> NO EXPERIENCE NECESSARY.
> *Apply Personnel,*
> *The Hudsucker Building*

*As we hear the coffee-shop door opening offscreen, a draft wafts the sheet
of newspaper off the counter and out of frame.*

SKYLINE

*We are again looking through the boardroom window as, offscreen, the
reporting executive drones on.*

> EXECUTIVE
> . . . Now then. O & O's. Our owned-and-operateds are
> performing far above expectations both here and abroad, and the
> Federal Tax Act of 1958 is giving us a swell write-off on our plant

and heavies . . .

Waring Hudsucker has been looking dreamily out the window. His attention returns to the droning executive, and the benignant smile returns to his lips.

. . . The news in the money market isn't good – it's excellent. D & B has reconfirmed us as Triple-A, and our last debenture issue was the year's fastest seller . . .

CITY STREET

We are following Norville, who walks dejectedly down the street, hands shoved into his pockets.

A sheet of newspaper eddies into frame. The wind tosses it this way and that.

Slap! – it plasters against another pedestrian, who bats it away.

The newspaper eddies around, then – slap! – plasters against Norville.

He peels it off and is about to toss it away but stops, noticing something.

NEWSPAPER SCRAP

It is a section of the want ads. One entry is perfectly circled by a coffee stain.

BACK TO NORVILLE

He looks up from the paper. There is purpose in his gaze. Wind whips his hair.

THE BOARDROOM

As the executive drones on, Waring Hudsucker is carefully winding his pocketwatch.

EXECUTIVE

. . . Our nominees and assigns continue to multiply and expand, extending our influence regionally, nationally and abroad. So third quarter and year-to-date, we've set a new record in sales . . .

Hudsucker looks up from his watch, smiles, runs his palms back over his fringe of hair.

. . . new record in gross . . .

Hudsucker tugs his sleeve cuffs to expose just the right amount.

. . . new record in pre-tax earnings . . .

Hudsucker takes a puff from his cigar and carefully sets it in his ashtray.

. . . new record in after-tax profit . . .

Hudsucker consults his pocketwatch.

The sweep second hand is starting the last revolution that will end precisely at noon.

. . . and our stock has split twice this year . . .

Hudsucker lays the watch carefully on the table.

. . . In short . . .

Savoring a pause, the reporting executive looks around the table.

. . . we're loaded.

This draws an appreciative chuckle from the board. It is cut off by:

HUDSUCKER
Ahem . . .

The board turns expectantly to Hudsucker in the foreground. Beyond him, the length of the boardroom table leads to the large picture window. Slowly, deliberately, Hudsucker rises to his feet and rubs his palms.

He swings his chair out. The board watches.

He steps up onto the chair. The board watches.

He steps up from the chair onto the board table. The heads of the board members swing up in unison.

Hudsucker is framed from mid-torso down. He shakes the tension loose from each leg, then waggles both arms, like an athlete preparing for a sprint.

II

ANOTHER EXECUTIVE
   . . . Mr Hudsucker?

CLOSE ON WANT ADS

The coffee-circled ad:

>THE FUTURE IS NOW
>*Start building yours at*
>*Hudsucker Industries.*
>*Low pay. Long Hours.*
>NO EXPERIENCE NECESSARY.
>*Apply Personnel,*
>*The Hudsucker Building*

The hand holding the paper drops away and we tilt up as Norville walks away into the background, toward an office building across the street. Lettering incised above its doorway identifies it as THE HUDSUCKER BUILDING.

We continue tilting up the length of the skyscraper to reveal a huge clock capping its facade. Above the clock is the identification HUDSUCKER INDUSTRIES. *Below the clock is the motto* THE FUTURE IS NOW.

The huge clock's sweep second hand is just approaching the position that will make the time 12:00 sharp.

As the second hand hits the twelve, the clock tolls, the boardroom window shatters, and Waring Hudsucker comes flying out.

HUDSUCKER
AAAAAAAAHHHHHHHH . . .

SECRETARIAL AREA

Somewhere in the Hudsucker Building a secretary sits typing next to an open window. Finished pages sit stacked beside her. As we hear another toll of the clock –

HUDSUCKER
aaaaaAAAAAAAAaaaaaahhh . . .

– Waring Hudsucker shoots past the window. His draft sends the stack of

papers wafting this way and that.

TRACKING

The building slips by behind Hudsucker as we drop laterally with him.
He yells, calmly running his palms back over his fringe of hair.

The clock tolls.

A HOTDOG VENDER

Down on the street an aproned man hands a steaming frank to a customer,
who hands him change. As we hear the approaching Hudsucker, both
men look up.

The clock tolls.

PASSER-BY ON SIDEWALK

The man, wearing a fedora, is in the foreground of an extreme low angle
whose background is the bottom three or four stories of the Hudsucker
Building.

The passer-by reacts to the approaching yell, looking up just as Hudsucker
enters.

Hudsucker plummets through the frame to his rendezvous with the
sidewalk, below frame.

DUTCH-ANGLE

The Hudsucker Building lists up into the distance. A woman in a fancy
fruited hat rises into frame at an opposing slant. Looking down at the
sidewalk, she sends two dismayed hands to her cheeks and
SCREEEEEEEEEAMS.

DISSOLVE THROUGH TO TOP FLOOR

As the last toll of the clock rings out, we are floating in toward the
shattered boardroom window. The woman's scream on the street below is
faint, echoing, mixing into the sound of an approaching siren.

Through the window we see the board members still sitting around the table, paralyzed in attitudes of horror and disbelief. All stare at the shattered window in the foreground.

At the end of the table Hudsucker's chair is empty and oddly askew. His cigar still smokes in its ashtray. There are dust footprints down the middle of the long oak table.

One executive sits with a pluming cigarette held halfway to his mouth. Another holds a carafe suspended on its way to his water glass. Another holds his spectacles inches from his nose.

We hear only the hum of the Hudsucker Clock.

Sid Mussburger enters frame. The only board member with the presence of mind to get up and look out the window, he is a man born to lead, or at least give orders.

He knocks a last piece of glass out of the sill with his knuckle, looks out, grunts, and draws his head back in.

The camera follows him into the room. The other board members' heads swivel to watch him, all staring, searching desperately for some hint as to the fate of their fallen president. Apparently, some absurd hope still lingers.

At the far end of the table, Mussburger plucks the smoking cigar from the suicide's ashtray.

> MUSSBURGER
> Pity to waste a whole Monte Cristo.

The other board members unfreeze, their fears confirmed.

> MOPING EXECUTIVE
> He could've opened the window.

> ELDERLY EXECUTIVE
> Waring Hudsucker never did anything the easy way.

> SOBBING EXECUTIVE
> My God, why?! Why did he do it?! Things were going so well!

> MUSSBURGER
> What am I, a headshrinker? Maybe the man was unhappy.

SOBBING EXECUTIVE

He didn't *look* unhappy!

DRY EXECUTIVE

Yeah, well, he didn't look rich.

ELDERLY EXECUTIVE

Waring Hudsucker was never an easy man to figure out. He built this company with his bare hands. Every step he took was a step up. Except of course this last one.

MUSSBURGER

Sure sure, he was a swell fella, but when the president, chairman of the board and holder of 87 percent of the company's stock drops forty-four floors –

PRECISE EXECUTIVE

Forty-five –

THOUGHTFUL EXECUTIVE

– Counting the mezzanine –

MUSSBURGER

– then the company too has a problem. Stillson, what exactly is the disposition of Waring's stock?

All heads turn to Stillson, the man who had been delivering Waring Hudsucker's last report.

STILLSON

Well, as you know, Hud left no will and had no family. The company bylaws are quite clear in that event. His entire portfolio will be converted to common stock and will be sold over the counter as of the first of the fiscal year following his demise.

MUSSBURGER

Meaning?

STILLSON

Meaning simply that Waring's stock, and control of the company, will be available to the public on January 1st.

MUSSBURGER

You mean to tell me that any slob in a smelly T-shirt will be able

16

to buy Hudsucker stock?

STILLSON

The company bylaws are quite clear.

SOBBING EXECUTIVE

My God! You're animals! How can you discuss his stock when
the man has just leapt forty-five floors –

PRECISE EXECUTIVE

Forty-four –

THOUGHTFUL EXECUTIVE

– Not counting the mezzanine.

MUSSBURGER

Quit showboating, Addison, the man is gone. The question now
is whether we're going to let John Q. Public waltz in and buy *our*
company.

THOUGHTFUL EXECUTIVE

What're you suggesting, Sidney? Certainly *we* can't afford to buy
a controlling interest.

MUSSBURGER

Not while the stock is this strong. How long before Hud's paper
hits the market?

STILLSON

January 1st.

DRY EXECUTIVE

Thirty days.

MOPING EXECUTIVE

Four weeks.

EAGER EXECUTIVE

A month at the most.

MUSSBURGER

One month to make the blue-chip investment of the century look
like a round-trip ticket on the Titanic.

THOUGHTFUL EXECUTIVE
We play up the fact that Hud is dead.

ALL
LONG LIVE THE HUD!

MOPING EXECUTIVE
We depress the stock –

EAGER EXECUTIVE
– to the point where we can buy 50 percent.

PRECISE EXECUTIVE
Fifty-one –

THOUGHTFUL EXECUTIVE
– Not counting the mezzanine.

CAUTIOUS EXECUTIVE
It could work.

OPTIMISTIC EXECUTIVE
It should work.

PRACTICAL EXECUTIVE
It would work.

Mussburger is examining printout at a ticker-tape machine.

MUSSBURGER
It's working already. Waring Hudsucker is abstract art on
Madison Avenue. All we need now is a new president who will
inspire real panic in our stockholders.

ENTHUSIASTIC EXECUTIVE
Yeah, a puppet!

EAGER EXECUTIVE
A proxy!

YET ANOTHER EXECUTIVE
A pawn!

*Mussburger strides from the ticker-tape machine to Hudsucker's chair and
sinks into it. He takes a last puff from his cigar and savors an exhale.*

Sure sure. Some jerk we can really push around.

SWINGING STEEL DOORS

The doors, reading MAILROOM, *burst open before Norville. He now wears a mail clerk's leather apron imprinted* HUDSUCKER MAILROOM/ The Future Is Now. *He pushes a piled-high mail cart down an aisle of the hellish warren which is criss-crossed by pipes that emit hissing jets of steam.*

Norville is accompanied by an orientation agent who bellows at him over the clamor and roar of many men laboring in the bowels of a great corporation.

AGENT
YOU PUNCH IN AT 8:30 EVERY MORNING EXCEPT
YOU PUNCH IN AT 7:30 FOLLOWING A BUSINESS
HOLIDAY UNLESS IT'S A MONDAY AND THEN YOU
PUNCH IN AT EIGHT O'CLOCK! YOU PUNCH IN AT 7:45
WHENEVER WE WORK EXTENDED DAY AND YOU
PUNCH OUT AT THE REGULAR TIME UNLESS YOU'VE
WORKED THROUGH LUNCH!

NORVILLE
What's exte–

AGENT
PUNCH IN LATE – AND THEY DOCK YA!

People on either side of the aisle bellow at Norville and stuff envelopes and packages under his elbows, into his pockets, under his chin, between his clenched teeth.

FIRST SCREAMER
THIS GOES TO SEVEN! MR MATUSZAK! URGENT!

AGENT
INCOMING ARTICLES, GET A VOUCHER! OUTGOING
ARTICLES, PROVIDE A VOUCHER! MOVE ANY
ARTICLE WITHOUT A VOUCHER – AND THEY DOCK
YA!

TAKE THIS UP TO THE SECRETARIAL POOL ON
THREE! A.S.A.P.! DON'T BREAK IT!

AGENT
LETTER SIZE A GREEN VOUCHER! FOLDER SIZE A
YELLOW VOUCHER! PARCEL SIZE A MAROON
VOUCHER!

THIRD SCREAMER
THIS ONE'S FOR MORGATROSS! CHOP CHOP!

AGENT
WRONG COLOR VOUCHER – AND THEY DOCK YA!
SIX–SEVEN–EIGHT–SEVEN–ZERO–FOUR–NINER–
ALPHA–SLASH–SIX! THAT IS YOUR EMPLOYEE
NUMBER! IT WILL NOT BE REPEATED! WITHOUT
YOUR EMPLOYEE NUMBER YOU CANNOT CASH
YOUR PAYCHECK!

FOURTH SCREAMER
THIS GOES UP TO TWENTY-SEVEN! RETURN A
WAIVER! *DON'T COME BACK WITHOUT A SIGNED
WAIVER!*

AGENT
INTER-OFFICE MAIL IS CODE 37! *INTRA*-OFFICE MAIL
IS 37 DASH 3! OUTSIDE MAIL IS 3 DASH 37! CODE IT
WRONG – AND THEY DOCK YA!

FIFTH SCREAMER
I WAS SUPPOSED TO HAVE THIS ON TWENTY-EIGHT
TEN MINUTES AGO! COVER FOR ME!

AGENT
THIS HAS BEEN YOUR ORIENTATION! IS THERE
ANYTHING YOU DO NOT UNDERSTAND? IS THERE
ANYTHING YOU UNDERSTAND ONLY PARTIALLY? IF
YOU HAVE NOT BEEN FULLY ORIENTED – IF THERE
IS SOMETHING YOU DO NOT UNDERSTAND IN ALL
OF ITS PARTICULARS – YOU MUST FILE A
COMPLAINT WITH PERSONNEL! FILE A FAULTY

COMPLAINT – AND THEY DOCK YA!

LATER: NORVILLE

He stands in front of a shelf of cubbyholes. We follow his hand as he draws an 8 × 10 envelope across the line of alphabetized mail slots. The envelope is addressed to MAX KLOPPITT, JR.

Muttering to himself:

> NORVILLE
> . . . bring it down to fif(?) . . . fifteen . . . sign the voucher, uh, waiver . . . cover for Mr Anatole . . . he's a swell guy . . . Morgatross . . . He was on, uh, Kloppitt Kloppitt Kloppitt . . .

He coasts across the 'K' mail slots and finally comes to MAX KLOPPITT, SR. *His hand moves to the next slot,* MAX KLOPPITT, JR. *This slot is half the size of the others. The envelope will not fit.*

Norville frowns.

He is about to fold the envelope but notices something stamped in red on its face: DO NOT FOLD.

Norville frowns.

As he stares at the envelope, we see envelopes swishing across the foreground, whipping by in rapid succession, left to right.

ANCIENT SORTER

An old man sits at the adjacent shelf, sorting mail. Without looking up, and with a constant high-speed back-and-forth flicking of his right hand, he is whisking pieces of mail one by one out of the pile of mail he holds in his left.

ANCIENT SORTER'S SHELF

His letters fly furiously but neatly into their mail slots.

NORVILLE

He raises his voice over the mailroom din:

NORVILLE
Say, what do you do when the envelope is too big for the slot?

The Ancient Sorter considers this as he continues whisking his mail.

ANCIENT SORTER
Well . . . if ya fold 'em, they fire ya . . .

Whisk. Whisk. Whisk.

. . . I usually throw 'em out.

Norville takes out a pencil and writes on the face of the envelope:

Dear Mr. Kloppitt,
Please give this letter to your son.
Thank you,
Norville Barnes

After a moment he adds:

Your friend in the mailroom.

He talks as he writes:

NORVILLE
Just got hired today!

ANCIENT SORTER
Terrific.

NORVILLE
Ya know, entry level!

ANCIENT SORTER
Tell me about it.

NORVILLE
I got big ideas, though!

ANCIENT SORTER
I'm sure you do.

NORVILLE

For instance, take a look at this sweet baby . . .

He takes an envelope from his pocket and hands it to the Ancient Sorter.

. . . You look like you can keep a secret . . .

The Ancient Sorter pulls a ragged piece of paper from the envelope. On the paper is a crudely drawn circle.

. . . Something I developed myself. Yessir, this is my ticket upstairs.

The Ancient Sorter looks questioningly from the circle to Norville, who explains:

. . . You know, for kids!

As Norville takes the paper back, the Ancient Sorter nods with feigned understanding.

ANCIENT SORTER

Terrific.

NORVILLE

So ya see, I won't be in the mailroom long.

ANCIENT SORTER
(*deadpan*)

Nooo, I don't guess you *will* be.

He resumes his sorting.

NORVILLE

How long've you been down here?

ANCIENT SORTER

Forty-eight years . . .

Whisk. Whisk.

. . . Next year they move me up to parcels . . .

Whisk. Whisk. Whisk.

. . . If I'm lucky.

A bell clangs.

23

The public-address system sputters to life.

PUBLIC ADDRESS

Attention Hudsucker employees. We regretfully announce that
at thirty seconds after the hour of noon, Hudsucker Time,
Waring Hudsucker, Founder, President, and Chairman of the
Board of Hudsucker Industries, merged with the infinite. To
mark this occasion of corporate loss, we ask that all employees
observe a moment of silent contemplation.

*All hubbub abruptly stops and the sounds of heavy machinery, hissing
steam pipes, and generators wind down to leave total silence.*

After a moment:

. . . Thank you for your kind attention. This moment has been
duly noted on your time cards and will be deducted from your
pay. That is all.

Machinery groans back into action and people return to their work just as:

A steam whistle screeches.

Alarm bells go off.

From the public-address system:

'Blue Letter! Blue Letter!'

The mailroom is thrown into pandemonium.

VARIOUS VOICES

Blue Letter! . . . It's a Blue Letter! . . . They're bringing down a
Blue Letter!

*One man spins to face the camera, his hands pressed over his ears. Steam
jets and hisses behind him.*

MAN

Blue Letter!

For the first time, the Ancient Sorter is animated:

ANCIENT SORTER

Jumpin' Jehosephat, a Blue Letter!

Mail carts and other paraphernalia are abruptly swept out of the crowded

24

aisle to form a clear path running down to an elevator in the background.

A light above the elevator goes on as sirens whoop. The elevator door sweeps open. It reveals a wall into which a four-foot-high hinged door is set.

This door swings open, and a dwarf emerges from the blinding light of the elevator interior. It is Old Man Hutchinson, the boss of the mailroom. He holds high a letter.

He takes loping dwarfstrides down the aisle.

We track in close shot on the letter as Hutchinson bears it along, passing faces alternately fearful and agog.

The Ancient Sorter is leaning over to whisper into Norville's ear:

> ANCIENT SORTER
> It's a Blue Letter . . . top, top level . . . confidential
> communication between the brass . . . usually bad news . . . they
> hate Blue Letters upstairs . . . Hate 'em!

25

You!

Norville looks over his shoulder, but the Ancient Sorter has disappeared.

. . . Yeah, you! BARNES!

As he points, the people around Norville shrink away.

. . . You don't look busy! Think you can handle a *Blue Letter*?

Norville gulps.

. . . This letter was sent down this morning by the big guy himself! Ats right, Waring Hudsucker! It's addressed to Sid Mussburger! Hudsucker's right-hand man! It's a Blue Letter! That means you put it right in Mussburger's hand. No secretaries! No receptionists! No colleagues! No excuses!

We track in on Hutchinson as he thrusts the Blue Letter into Norville's face. We can see the veins in his eyes, the veins in his nose, the hairs in his ears.

. . . *MUSSBURGER*!

ELEVATOR DOORS

They sweep open and we move in on the young elevator operator, who leers into the camera. He wears a brass-buttoned uniform, white gloves and a pillbox hat. The name BUZZ *is stitched onto his breast pocket.*

As Norville enters the elevator:

BUZZ

Hiya, buddy! The name is Buzz, I got the fuzz . . .

He lifts his pillbox hat to reveal a white crewcut, then lets the elastic chin-strap snap the cap back down into place.

. . . I make the elevator do what she does!

He holds out his hand, but as Norville reaches to shake it he snaps it away and pats down his crewcut.

. . . Hang it up to dry.

26

He cackles and powers the elevator into gear. Norville's knees buckle under a huge upward surge.

. . . What's your pleasure, buddy?

NORVILLE

Forty-fourth floor, and it's very –

BUZZ

Forty-four, the top-brass floor say buddy! What takes fifty years to get up to the top floor and thirty seconds to get down?

NORVILLE

I –

BUZZ

Waring Hudsucker! Na-ha-ha-ha-ha! Say buddy!

With a powerful down-shifting sound Buzz brakes the elevator and opens the door. Three people enter.

BUZZ

Mr Kline, up to nine. Mrs Dell, personnel. Mr Levin, thirty-seven.

MR LEVIN

Thirty-six.

BUZZ

Walk down. Ladies and gentlemen, step to the rear – here comes gargantuan Mr Grier.

An obese man enters, nodding acknowledgment:

FAT MAN

Buzz.

Buzz throws the doors shut and sends the elevator into its power-rise.

BUZZ

Say buddy! Who's the most liquid businessman on The Street?

NORVILLE

Well, I –

BUZZ

Waring Hudsucker! Na-ha-ha-ha-ha! Say buddy! When is the sidewalk fully dressed? When it's 'wearing' Hudsucker! Na-ha-ha-ha!

He turns to look at Norville.

. . . Ya get it buddy, it's a pun, it's a knee-slapper, it's a play on Jesus, Joseph and Mary, is that a Blue Letter?!

All heads in the elevator turn, aghast, to look, and those near Norville shrink away.

. . . Cripes a'mighty, whyn't ya tell a guy?! Hold on folks, we're express to the top floor!

The elevator screams into overdrive.

ELEVATOR DOORS

Sweeping open. Norville staggers out.

BUZZ
(*hissing*)

Good luck, buddy!

The doors sweep shut. Norville looks nervously around.

Behind him the elevator doors suddenly open again.

BUZZ

– You're gonna need it!

The elevator doors slam shut and we hear its engines scream as the elevator power-dives away.

Norville turns toward the executive offices.

Plush, thick-carpeted silence.

A scraping sound stands out in the high-powered executive quiet. Norville looks to one side.

A workman in painter's overalls squats in front of a pair of heavy oak doors. With a razor blade he is scraping off the name WARING HUDSUCKER.

NORVILLE

. . . Mr Mussburger's office?

The scraper looks sullenly back over his shoulder. With a jerk of his thumb he indicates the direction.

Norville enters the adjacent office.

OUTER OFFICE

Two secretaries are in Mussburger's reception office. The first is a filing secretary who stands frozen in the foreground, her hand poised over an open drawer to deposit a folder, as she stares at Norville with an amused and supercilious sneer.

The second secretary, also a gargoyle, is seated behind a desk in the background that flanks the door to Mussburger's private office. She sits with her hands clasped on the desk, staring at Norville with the hunch-shouldered look of a patient vulture.

SECRETARY

Do you have an appointment?

Uhh, no, I –

Shall we look in the book, hmmmmmmmmm?

She opens an enormous leather-bound book with crinkly yellow pages.

NORVILLE
No ma'am, ya see, I wouldn't be in the –

SECRETARY
We don't seem to be in the boooook.

Norville is groping in his apron pocket.

NORVILLE
No ma'am, ya see I don't have an –

SECRETARY
If we had an appointment we'd be in the booook.

NORVILLE
I know, but you see I have this – here it is, this letter –

A low, unearthly wail fills the room, the sound of a million souls moaning in purgatory.

The secretary looks –

FAST TRACK IN

– at the sneering file secretary, who sneers no more. Her mouth is stretched wide as she wails and points –

FAST TRACK IN

– at the Blue Letter that Norville innocently holds, and –

BACK TO TRACK IN ON WAILING SECRETARY

– the wail becomes deafening as we track into her mouth and the screen goes black and:

CLICK

The blackness and the wailing are both cut short by the sound of a door opening. We are inside Mussburger's office as its door swings in to admit Norville.

Behind him, in the outer office, the filing secretary is slumped back motionless in a chair, a damp rag draped across her forehead. The other secretary fans her with a towel.

The door closes behind Norville.

We hear a rhythmic click-click-click and the hum of ventilation.

NORVILLE'S POV

Across miles of carpet is a huge desk behind which a large chair sits swivelled away toward the window. From above the back of the chair cigar smoke wreathes up. A telephone cord snakes around to the seated man, hidden from view. On the desktop is a perpetual-motion gizmo of swinging ball bearings going click-click-click.

Mussburger's voice is irritable, punctuated by listening silences:

> MUSSBURGER
> Gambotz? . . . Harry Gambotz? No, he's green but he's not slow . . .

A ticker-tape machine stutters and burps in the far corner of the office.

> . . . No no, they moved him over to Grommets and O-Rings, he's doing pretty well there . . .

A huge mechanical arm – the sweep second hand of the Hudsucker Clock on the facade of the building – rumbles by immediately outside the window, casting a shadow that slithers across the office.

> . . . Sure sure, Parkinson's stupid but he's ambitious, too hard to control . . .

Mussburger swivels to face Norville, who stands deferentially at the door. Still listening at the phone, Mussburger waves him forward.

> . . . No! Not McClanahan; sure he bungled the Teleyard merger, but that means he's got something to prove . . .

31

He covers the mouthpiece.

. . . Who let you in?

NORVILLE

I –

MUSSBURGER
(into the phone)

Atwater? Tremendous. Except I fired him last week –

The intercom buzzes fiercely.

INTERCOM

Mr Bumstead is waiting downstairs.

Mussburger hits the intercom.

MUSSBURGER

Tell him I'll be right there.

He looks at Norville.

. . . Well, spit it out.

NORVILLE

I –

Mussburger is already answering the tinny voice issuing from the phone:

MUSSBURGER

Yeah, maybe *you're* the company's biggest moron. We can't use
Morris, he's been with us too long, nice guy, too many friends.
Matter of fact, why don't you fire him? No – scratch that; *I'll* fire
him.

He looks up at Norville.

. . . Make it fast, huh – fast.

NORVILLE

You –

The intercom squawks.

INTERCOM

Mr Bumstead is growing restless –

32

I'll be right there. Give him a magazine.

To Norville:

. . . What're you, a mute?

The second phone on Mussburger's desk rings.

. . . Yeah, how's the stock doing? . . . Bad, huh? Well it's not bad enough!

Into the first phone:

. . . Look, chump, either you find me a grade-A ding-dong or you can tender your key to the executive washroom.

Into the second phone:

. . . And that goes double for you.

Into the first phone:

. . . Ear-clay?

Into both phones:

. . . Ood-gay!

He slams down both phones. He looks at Norville.

. . . This better be good. I'm in a bad mood.

Norville clears his throat.

Well, sir, I've got something for you from the mailroom, but first if I could just take a minute or so from your very busy time . . .

He reaches into his mailroom apron and hands a scrap of paper across the desk to Mussburger, who stares, frozen, at Norville, making no move to take the paper.

. . . to show you a, uh . . .

Norville, undaunted, displays his drawing.

. . . a little something I've been working on for the last two or three years . . .

Mussburger's burning eyes finally shift momentarily to look at the crudely drawn circle. He looks incredulously back at Norville.

. . . You know, for kids! Which is perfect for Hudsucker – not that I claim to be any great genius; like they say, inspiration is 99 percent perspiration, and in my case it's at least twice that, but I gotta tell ya, Mr Mussburger, sir, this sweet baby –

MUSSBURGER

WAIT A MINUTE!

With one last click the perpetual-motion ball bearings obediently halt.

As Mussburger's eyes burn in on him, Norville stands mute and paralyzed.

His eyes locked on Norville's, Mussburger circles the desk. He stands toe-to-toe with Norville.

He thrusts his face into Norville's, whose head moves reflexively back. Mussburger's nose is an inch from Norville's, his eyes burning, searching, studying, evaluating.

Finally he draws his head back.

MUSSBURGER

Hmmmm . . .

With one hand he thrusts his cigar into Norville's gaping mouth. With the other hand he raises Norville's chin so that his teeth clench on the cigar.

MUSSBURGER

Umm-hmm . . .

He steps back, eyes still on Norville, and jerks his thumb over his shoulder, indicating the chair behind his desk.

MUSSBURGER

Siddown.

Norville, his lips puckered around the unaccustomed cigar, looks bemusedly from the chair to Mussburger.

. . . Go ahead. Try it on.

Norville obeys, reluctantly, stiffly.

. . . Put your feet up.

Norville is again reluctant.

. . . Go ahead.

Norville obeys. Mussburger studies.

. . . Let's get to know one another, shall we?

Norville's eyes squint against the cigar smoke wreathing from between his teeth. Mussburger seems to relax.

. . . Let's chat!

He beams.

. . . Man to man!

Norville beams.

. . . You weren't blessed with much . . .

He waves vaguely toward his head and searches for a euphemism.

. . . *education*, were you?

NORVILLE
Well, I'm a college graduate.

MUSSBURGER
All right, but you didn't *excel* in your studies?

NORVILLE
Well, I made the dean's list.

MUSSBURGER
(*worried*)
Hmmm.

Norville sputters out cigar smoke.

NORVILLE
At the Muncie College of Business Administration.

MUSSBURGER
(*relieved*)
Sure sure. And did your classmates there call you 'jerk' or . . .

He searches.

. . . 'schmoe'?

Norville shakes his head.

. . . 'Shnook'? 'Dope'? 'Dipstick'? 'Lamebrain'?

NORVILLE
No sir.

MUSSBURGER
Not even behind your back?

NORVILLE
Sir! They voted me most likely to succeed!

MUSSBURGER
You're fired.

NORVILLE
But sir! –

MUSSBURGER
Get your feet off my desk.

NORVILLE
But –

MUSSBURGER
Get out of my sight.

Norville, squinting against the cigar smoke, pulls the cigar out of his mouth as he doubles forward, feet still up, groping for a place for the cigar. He sets it blindly on a loose stack of papers.

MUSSBURGER
My God! The Bumstead contracts!

NORVILLE
Oh my God, sir!

The top page radiates a crinkling circle of incipient flame from the cigar's

38

live end.

MUSSBURGER

You nitwit! I worked for three years on this deal!

NORVILLE

Oh my God, sir!

Norville picks up the top page and wildly fans it, whereupon it bursts into flame.

MUSSBURGER

I'll take care of it. Just get out!

Norville dumps the burning page into a wastebasket, the contents of which ignite.

NORVILLE

Oh my God, sir!

His desk hides the wastebasket from Mussburger, who is flipping angrily through the remaining pages of the Bumstead contracts.

MUSSBURGER

Why, you nitwit. You almost destroyed the most sensitive deal of my career!

Norville, behind him, runs frantically toward a water-cooler at the far end of the office.

The intercom buzzes.

INTERCOM

Sir, Mr Bumstead is threatening to leave the building.

MUSSBURGER

I'm on my way down. We need the first page of the contracts retyped with carbons to legal affairs.

Behind him Norville wraps his arms around the glass water tank and pulls it off its base. He staggers back across the vast expanse of office toward the desk, hugging the tank whose water gloob-gloobs out its open bottom and splashes down over his knees.

NORVILLE

Oh my God, sir!

He reaches the wastebasket just as the last bit of water escapes the tank. He shakes the empty tank over the flames and then tosses it to the floor where – CRASH – it shatters.

> MUSSBURGER

Out of this office. OUT!

He answers a ringing phone:

> . . . How's the stock doing?

> NORVILLE

Oh my God, sir!

Norville sprints to a window and runs both palms over it, desperately seeking a way to open it.

> MUSSBURGER

Down three points, huh?

He notices Norville scrabbling at the window, which does not open.

> – Not that way! Through the door!

> NORVILLE

Oh my God, sir!

The intercom buzzes.

> INTERCOM

Sir, Secretarial reports that it will take three hours to retype the Bumstead contracts, and Mr Bumstead is threatening to leave the –

> MUSSBURGER

Not the whole contract, just the first page!

Norville runs by on his way back to the wastebasket.

> . . . What're you doing? Out of here! OUT!

> NORVILLE

Oh my God, sir!

Norville furiously stomps on the flames in the wastebasket and – his foot sticks. Further stomping only makes the flaming wastebasket roar up and down with his foot.

INTERCOM

But he's threatening to leave the –

MUSSBURGER

I'll be there!

INTERCOM

– and your wife has been trying to reach you.

Norville hops and kicks, but the wastebasket stays in place. He drops to the floor to try to wrench the flaming wastebasket off his foot.

MUSSBURGER

Up on your feet! We don't crawl at Hudsucker Industries!

NORVILLE

Sir, my leg is on fire!

Norville finally pries the wastebasket loose. Now the problem is what to do with it.

With a bark, Mussburger answers his insistently ringing second phone.

MUSSBURGER

Yeah!

An offended matronly voice responds:

PHONE

I beg your pardon!

Behind Mussburger, Norville picks up the flaming trash receptacle and hot-potatoes it toward the window.

NORVILLE

Oh my God, sir!

MUSSBURGER

Hello dear.

Norville throws the basket at the closed window. The glass shatters and the flaming basket plummets to oblivion.

A ferocious draft roars through the office.

On Mussburger's desk, the remaining pages of the Bumstead contracts are sucked away.

MUSSBURGER

My God! The Bumstead contracts!

NORVILLE

Oh my God, sir!

Mussburger lunges for the contracts as they are sucked out the window.

He runs, jumps onto the sill, grabs – his fist clenches around one wafting page – he is about to fall –

MUSSBURGER

EEEEEAAAAAHHHHH!

EXECUTIVE WAITING ROOM

Bumstead, a short, fat, heavily perspiring executive, is screaming at an offscreen secretary. He holds a pot of coffee in one hand and a copy of Boy's Life *in the other.*

In the window behind him we see loose sheets of paper fluttering by.

BUMSTEAD

No magazine. No coffee. MUSSBURGER! I wanna see MUSSBURGER! Or did he jump out a window too?!

NORVILLE

Desperately hanging onto Mussburger by his legs.

NORVILLE

Don't worry, Mr Mussburger! I gotcha! I gotcha by your pants!

MUSSBURGER

Dangling upside-down. Norville's cry prompts a thinking squint.

MUSSBURGER

. . . Pants . . .

HE REMEMBERS (*the screen goes watery*):

A basement tailor shop. Luigi, a kindly Italian tailor, is running a measuring tape up Mussburger's inseam.

> LUIGI
>
> Meester Moosaburger, I give-a you pants a nice-a dooble stitch. Make 'em strong, and they look-a real sharp.

> MUSSBURGER
>
> No! Single stitch is fine.

> LUIGI
>
> But please-a Meester Moosaburger, the dooble stitch she last-a forever –

> MUSSBURGER
>
> Why on earth would I need a double stitch? To pad your bill? Single stitch is fine!

BACK TO DANGLING MUSSBURGER

> MUSSBURGER
>
> Damn!

We hear a loud tearing sound as Mussburger drops a few inches.

QUICK WIPE TO LUIGI AT HIS SEWING-MACHINE

He muses as he works:

> LUIGI
>
> What the heck. Meester Moosaburger sooch a nice-a guy, I give him dooble steech-a anyway. Assa some-a strong-a steech-a, you bet!

BACK TO MUSSBURGER'S PANTS

The tearing fabric abruptly catches and stops; the pants now hold intact.

MUSSBURGER

Sighing with relief.

He looks up.

NORVILLE

His arms are wrapped around Mussburger's ankles; the heels of Mussburger's shoes dig into his face.

MUSSBURGER

Looking. Thinking.

NORVILLE

Struggling to hold on.

MUSSBURGER

Contemplating.

MUSSBURGER

Hmmm . . .

He absently removes a cigar from his breast pocket and sticks it in his mouth. He holds his lighter under the cigar, not noticing that the flame points the wrong way.

He looks at Norville.

NORVILLE

Face drawn with effort, still struggling to hang on. A pull back from the close shot reveals, however, that Norville's arms are now wrapped around – emptiness. Mussburger's legs are gone.

Norville throws his head back and laughs, it seems, insanely – but the continuing pull back shows that Norville is merely pantomiming the adventure for the benefit of the board members, Mussburger included. They stand around Mussburger's office, laughing gaily. All safe now, no harm done. This inaugurates:

THE LAUGHING MONTAGE

Norville is entertaining the board with his depiction of the near-disaster.

Mussburger slaps him merrily on the back.

CLOSE SHOT: BOARD MEMBER LAUGHING

ANOTHER BOARD MEMBER LAUGHING

MUSSBURGER LAUGHING

NORVILLE LAUGHING

FREEZE FRAME

On Norville's laughing face.

We pull back to reveal that the frozen picture is a newspaper photo on the front page of the Manhattan Argus. *Its headline reads:* UNTRIED YOUTH TO HELM HUDSUCKER. *The subhead reads: Stockholders Wary. The sub-subhead reads: Meteoric Rise from Mailroom.*

The continued pull back reveals that we are looking at the newspaper over someone's shoulder. The person swivels around and, his face now to us, we see that it is Norville. He throws his head back and laughs merrily.

As he laughs – THWOCK – *a steaming towel is thrown onto his face and he continues to swivel. The continuing pull back shows that he is in a barber chair.*

His head drops back and out of frame as the swivelling chair is cranked down, but immediately – still spinning –

– his head reappears as the chair is cranked up again. Still laughing, Norville is now freshly shaven and has a slicked-back haircut, heavy with pomade.

FREEZE

On Norville's laughing face.

Pull back to reveal it is another front-page photo next to a new headline: MAN FROM MUNCIE SPOOKS WALL STREET. *The subhead: Hud Board Rolling Dice on 'Fresh Ideas'.*

Continued pull back reveals that the paper is lying on a chair. Norville's mailroom apron is tossed onto the chair to cover it.

Pan to where the apron was tossed from. Norville stands on a tailor's stage, laughing, as the tailor, also laughing, takes his measurements.

Norville, in shirtsleeves, boxer shorts, hose stockings and garters, is surrounded by board members who laugh with him.

The tailor merrily throws up his arms and spreads wide his measuring tape.

We swish to a board member, laughing merrily, arms also thrown wide, ticker tape stretching between his hands. We are now in the Hudsucker boardroom, where the assembled board members roar with laughter. The executive at the ticker-tape machine festively tosses the tape.

It lands on a pile of previously discharged tape, but a pan up reveals that we are now in Mussburger's office. As his ticker-tape machine continues to chatter we track toward Mussburger, who sits behind his desk reading a newspaper, laughing.

On his desk the perpetual ball bearings swing; outside his window the second hand of the Hudsucker Clock rumbles by, sweeping a shadow across the floor. Evil prevails.

As Mussburger reads the inside of the newspaper, our continued track in shows its front-page headline: HUD STOCK DROPPING. *Subhead: When Will 'Fresh Ideas' Bear Fruit?*

We track in on the front-page photo: Norville laughing, his chin propped in his hand.

The photograph comes to life as Norville unfreezes, laughing.

We are now pulling back from Norville, who sits behind a huge oak desk, newly coiffed and tailored.

The continuing pull back leaves Norville looking quite small in a large, elegant office. His laughter echoes.

The laughter is winding down as if Norville, exhausted, has been at it for several days.

Double doors swing shut in the foreground. Gold letters say: OFFICE OF THE PRESIDENT. PRIVATE.

Beyond them, the muffled laughter dies.

FADE OUT

49

FADE IN: NEW YORK SKYLINE

In the skyline we can see the Hudsucker Building topped by the Hudsucker Clock.

A cigar enters frame in the foreground, then the face of the man smoking it. Gazing contemplatively at the Hudsucker Building, he takes a puff from his cigar and then plucks it from his mouth and waves it, as if painting a headline.

MAN

'The Einstein of Enterprise.' 'The Edison of Industry.' 'The Billion-Dollar Cranium.' . . . 'Idea Man.'

An explosion:

– And not one of you mugs has given me a story on him!

REVERSE

The editor's glassed-in office is filled with reporters. They are all veterans, and observe the rituals of the staff meeting with polite boredom.

Through the glass walls beyond them we can see the furious activity of an army of reporters, editors and copy boys waging the never-ending battle to put out a quality daily newspaper.

The editor slams a newspaper onto his desk in disgust.

. . . Facts, figures, charts! They never sold a newspaper! I read this morning's edition of the *Argus* and let me tell you something: I'd wrap a fish in it! I'd use it as kindling! Hell, I'd even train my poodle with it if he wasn't a French poodle and more partial to the pages of Paree Soir! But I sure wouldn't shell out a hard-earned nickel to *read* the dadblamed thing!

REPORTER ONE

Come on, Chief, give us a break.

CHIEF

Suuuure, Tibbs, take a break! Go to Florida! Lie in the sun, wait for a coconut to drop, file a story on it – it'd be more of a grabber than your piece on the Commie grain surplus! The Human Angle! That's what sells papers! We need a front page with heart,

50

and the whole idea of the 'Idea Man' idea can put it there!

REPORTER TWO

Chief, if we had more access –

CHIEF

Yeah, and if a frog had wings he wouldn't bump his ass a-hoppin'! I don't want excuses, I want results!

WHACK! –

Without looking at it the editor has slammed down the lid of the cigar box on his desk, toward which one reporter's hand had been cautiously reaching.

The reporter jerks his fingers away and the editor spares the briefest moment to glare at him.

. . . I wanna know what makes the Idea Man tick! Where is he from? Where is he going? I wanna know everything about this guy! Has he got a girl? Has he got parents?

REPORTER THREE

Everybody has parents.

All right, how many? How 'bout it, Parkinson, you've been awful quiet over there.

PARKINSON

Uhhh . . .

REPORTER NEXT TO PARKINSON

Still waters run deep, Chief.

CHIEF

The only thing that runs deep with Parkinson is the holes in his ears. Yes, the Idea Man! What're his hopes and dreams, his desires and aspirations? Does he think all the time or does he set aside a certain portion of the day? How tall is he and what's his shoe size? Where does he sleep and what does he eat for breakfast? Does he put jam on his toast or doesn't he put jam on his toast, and if not why not and since when?

He looks Socratically about.

. . . Well?!

No answer.

. . . Ahh, you're useless. Yes, Idea Man! Creator! Innovator! Cerebrator! –

WOMAN'S VOICE

Fake.

CHIEF

Huhh!

THE WOMAN

Star reporter Amy Archer – attractive, smartly dressed.

AMY

I tell ya the guy's a phony.

CHIEF

Phony, huh?

                              AMY
As a three-dollar bill.

                              CHIEF
Says who?

                              AMY
Says me, Amy Archer. Why is he an Idea Man – because
Hudsucker says he is? What're his ideas? Why won't they let
anyone interview him? . . .

One reporter is leaning into another to keep his voice low:

                            REPORTER
Five bucks says she mentions her Pulitzer.

                        THE OTHER REPORTER
Again? You're on.

                              AMY
                   (*as she picks up the morning paper*)
Why won't they let us interview him? Genius my eye – why
won't they tell us a single solitary thing about him? And just take
a look at the mug on this guy – the jutting eyebrows, the simian
forehead, the idiotic grin. Why he has a face only a mother could
love –

WHACK! *The editor has again slammed down the cigar-box lid, but:*

*Amy, smiling, raises a cigar into frame. She tosses it to the reporter whose
reach was too slow.*

– On payday! The only story here is how this guy made a monkey
out of *you*, Al.

                              CHIEF
Yeah, well, monkey or not I'm still editor of this rag. Amy, I
thought you were doing that piece on the FBI – J. Edgar
Hoover: When Will He Marry?

                              AMY
I filed it yesterday.

                              CHIEF
Well, do a follow-up: Hoover: Crimebuster Or Pantywaist? And

                               54

the rest of you bums get up off your brains and get me that Idea Man story!

REPORTERS

All right, Chief . . . We'll do our best, Chief . . . I'll give it a shot, Chief . . .

Amy strides to the door.

AMY

Al, he's the bunk.

SLAM!

One of the wagering reporters grins at the other, who is taking out a five-dollar bill.

The door bursts open and Amy sticks her head in.

. . . I'll stake my Pulitzer on it!

ELEVATOR DOORS

They sweep open to reveal the leering face of Buzz, the elevator gnat.

BUZZ

Say buddy! Where'd ya get the new duds?

Norville is entering the elevator in his new executive outfit.

. . . And say buddy, how'd old bucketbutt like his Blue Letter? Na-ha-ha-ha-ha! Did he bust a gut? Did he die? Did he – Well, hello, Mr Mussburger sir.

As Mussburger enters the elevator, Buzz is instant decorum.

. . . How're you this fine morning, sir?

Norville has been worriedly patting at his pockets since the mention of the Blue Letter.

NORVILLE

That reminds me, Mr Mu– uh, Sid. I never did give you that –

MUSSBURGER

Lobby. We haven't got all day.

BUZZ

Right away, Mr Mussburger sir.

As he talks, Mussburger pats at his suit pocket, takes out a cigar, inspects it.

MUSSBURGER

Well I'm starved. I understand it'll be quite an affair this afternoon, and the executive roast tom turkey at the Bohemian Grove redefines the word superb.

He puts the cigar in his mouth, and Buzz's hand is there with a lighter.

BUZZ

My pleasure, sir.

NORVILLE

Roast tom turkey. Mm-mm –

MUSSBURGER

Sure sure . . .

The elevator doors open.

BUZZ

It's been a pleasure serving you, Mr Mussburger.

Buzz turns to Norville, puzzled but trying to hide it:

. . . And it's been a pleasure serving you too, uh . . . buddy.

Mussburger is already striding through the lobby; Norville lopes to catch up.

NORVILLE

Say Mr Muss– . . . uh, Sid – shouldn't we be a little bit concerned with the downward spiral of our stock these last few days? I mean, you're the expert, but at the Muncie College of Business Administration they told us –

Mussburger gives an artificially hearty laugh and claps Norville on the shoulder.

MUSSBURGER

Relax, Norville. It's only natural in a period of transition for the
more timid element to run for cover.

NORVILLE

Okay, Sid. Like I said, you're the expert, but . . .

SIDEWALK

Norville is still loping behind Mussburger as they exit the building.

NORVILLE

. . . you don't happen to remember the plan I outlined to you the
day I set fire to your off– . . . uh, the day I was promoted?

MUSSBURGER

I do remember, and I was impressed. Anyway, that's all
forgotten now. Driver!

NORVILLE

Thank you, Sid, but the reason I mention it is, it would require
such a small capital investment – again, you're the expert here –

MUSSBURGER

Dammit, where's my car!

NORVILLE

– but there's such an enormous potential profit-wise given the demographics – baby boom – discretionary income in the burgeoning middle class –

A black limousine pulls up.

MUSSBURGER

About time.

NORVILLE

– so, if you think it's appropriate, I'd like to bounce the idea off a few people at lunch.

Mussburger is getting into the back seat –

MUSSBURGER

Sure, sure, tell whoever you want . . .

– and, to Norville's surprise, slamming the door shut behind him.

. . . and I'd like to hear about it at some point too.

SCREEEECH *– the car pulls away. Norville is left talking to himself on the empty sidewalk.*

NORVILLE

But Sid, I thought you and I were . . .

DOORMAN

Say bud, could you keep the sidewalk clear here?

NORVILLE

But I'm the president of this – aww, forget it!

COFFEE SHOP

It is a cheap place a half-flight down from the street. We are looking across an elbow of the counter. In the middle background Norville sits dejectedly stirring a cup of coffee.

Behind him, through the window wells, we see the back-and-forth feet of pedestrians bustling by on the sidewalk.

In the extreme foreground sit two steaming mugs of coffee. They belong to two veterans of the coffee shop who, from offscreen, narrate the scene.

> VETERAN ONE

I got gas, Benny.

> VETERAN TWO

Yeah, tell me about it.

> VETERAN ONE

No kiddin', Benny. I got gas.

> VETERAN TWO

Ya get the special?

> VETERAN ONE

Fah from it . . .

He gives a low whistle as a woman enters from the street and hesitates by the door, looking around. Still attractive but now looking somewhat down-at-the-heels, it is Amy Archer.

. . . Enter the dame.

> VETERAN TWO

There's one in every story.

> VETERAN ONE

Ten bucks says she's looking for a handout.

> VETERAN TWO

Twenty bucks says not here she don't find one.

> VETERAN ONE

She's looking for her mark.

Amy's eyes settle on Norville, and she heads for the empty stool next to his.

> VETERAN TWO

She finds him.

> VETERAN ONE

She sits down.

Amy says something to the counter waitress, who exits.

> VETERAN TWO
> . . . And awduhs a light lunch.

> VETERAN ONE
> She looks in her purse . . .

She is holding her wallet upside down.

> VETERAN TWO
> . . . No money. How will she pay for this lunch?

> VETERAN ONE
> The mark notices.

Norville, however, is not noticing: he is staring intently at his coffee spoon, his hat pushed back on his head, his other hand propping up a cheekbone. Amy's presence does not seem to have registered.

> VETERAN TWO
> . . . He's not noticing, Benny.

> VETERAN ONE
> Maybe he's wise.

VETERAN TWO
He don't look wise.

VETERAN ONE
Plan two: here come the waterworks.

Amy starts crying.

VETERAN TWO
Yellowstone.

VETERAN ONE
Old Faithful.

VETERAN TWO
Hello Niagara.

VETERAN ONE
He notices.

*As Amy cries, she accidently-on-purpose jostles Norville and he finally
does indeed notice.*

VETERAN TWO
He's concerned.

*Amy mouths words at Norville, who reacts sympathetically and waves his
hands at the waitress.*

VETERAN ONE
She explains her predicament, and . . .

VETERANS ONE AND TWO IN UNISON
. . . entuh the light lunch.

The waitress is entering to set a plate of cottage cheese in front of Amy.

She continues to talk to Norville, smiling wanly.

VETERAN TWO
She's got other problems, of course . . .

VETERAN ONE
. . . her mother needs an operation . . .

VETERAN TWO
. . . adenoids.

VETERAN ONE

No, Benny: lumbago.

Veteran One's enunciation of 'lumbago' falls into perfect sync with Amy's moving lips.

Norville is listening sympathetically, but he suddenly notices his watch.

VETERAN ONE

She's losing him, Benny.

Norville is rising to his feet.

VETERAN TWO

Maybe he's wise.

VETERAN ONE

He don't look wise.

As Norville turns to leave:

VETERAN TWO

How does she pull this out?

She puts the back of her hand dramatically to her forehead.

Veteran One is disbelieving:

VETERAN ONE

She isn't!

Veteran Two is thrilled:

VETERAN TWO

She is!

And indeed she does – faint dead away, falling backwards on the stool so that Norville has no choice but to catch her.

Norville holds her awkwardly, looking around for help.

VETERAN ONE

She's good, Benny.

VETERAN TWO

She's *damn* good, Lou.

A waitress enters in the foreground to block our view of the action. She

faces us in a cropping that gives us only her torso and the steaming pot of coffee she holds as she inquires in a bored, nasal voice:

WAITRESS

Can I get you boys anything else?

REVERSE

The two veterans' faces, weathered by wide and wearying experience, are crowned by cabbie caps.

VETERAN ONE

Bromo.

Beat.

VETERAN TWO

. . . Bromo.

NORVILLE'S OUTER OFFICE

From inside we are looking at its frosted-glass door. Outside, the sign painter is just finishing lettering:

NORVILLE BARNES
President

The painter makes way as we see Norville's shadow approaching; even from inside the room we can hear that he is wheezing heavily. He is apparently carrying the woman cradled in his arms. He reaches down to get the doorknob, can't manage it, turns to press his back against the door and get the knob with his other hand.

Amy chatters away:

AMY

I'm sorry we had to take the stairs – it was just that horrible little elevator boy. At any rate, there I was, travelling the length and breadth of this great country; some I met were kind to me, others exceedingly cruel . . .

The door opens as Norville swings around to enter. He is wheezing like a gas main about to explode.

. . .Call me a tramp or hobo or vagabond or adventuress –
travelling by motorbus, rail, and even by thumb –

She langorously points:

. . . The couch please.

*Still wheezing noisily, Norville staggers over to the couch and gently
deposits her. He straightens up and looks at her.*

. . . hoarding every dollar, counting every nickel, pinching every
penny – yes, it's been a long road leading to that coffee shop
downstairs . . .

NORVILLE'S POV

*Amy is smiling wanly at the camera. The image pulsates as blood pounds
behind Norville's eyeballs. We hear the loud rasping of breath resonating
inside his head, an airy steam whistle, the pounding of surf. Amy's voice
is far away.*

NORVILLE

Just a minute.

*He perches drunkenly on the edge of the couch and puts his head between
his knees, fighting for breath.*

AMY

I don't know what came over me. I suppose it was the shock of
eating after so long without; the enzymes kicking in after so long,
or whatever. But then you couldn't possibly know what it is to be
tired and hungry –

NORVILLE

Hungry, anyway.

AMY

I don't want to bore you with all the sordid details of my life; it's
not a happy story . . .

Norville rises and starts putting throw pillows behind her head.

. . . Suffice it to say that I'm jobless, though not for want of
trying, that I'm friendless, with no one to – thank you – take care

of me, and that had you not come along at just exactly the
moment that you did –

She screams, staring down at the couch.

Norville jumps, startled, then follows her look.

On the white sofa cushion where he had been sitting is printed, in wet ink:

NORVILLE BARNES
President

AMY
Norville, I didn't know you were president here!

*Norville stares dumbfounded at the cushion. When the nickel finally drops
he twists around to look at the seat of his pants, on which is printed, in
wet ink:*

SENRAB ELLIVRON
tnediserP

Norville is bemused but still modest:

NORVILLE
Oh, it's nothing really. Just determination and hard work . . .

He unbuckles his trousers.

. . . Although when I started in the mailroom last Tuesday I
thought it might take more time –

Buzz enters holding a brown paper bag.

BUZZ
Say buddy, here's the whisky you asked f–

*He freezes, taking in the scene: Amy reclining on the couch; Norville
standing in front of her with his pants around his ankles, still breathing
heavily; the bottle of whiskey in his own hand.*

NORVILLE
(*flustered*)
Thank you, Buzz, just leave it on the credenza.

BUZZ
Happy days, buddy . . .

As he turns to leave:

. . . and I'll tell your secretary you're not to be disturbed.
Yowzuh!

He snaps the elastic strap under his chin and exits.

> AMY
> (*shuddering*)

What a horrible little person.

> NORVILLE

Oh, Buzz is pretty harmless, really –

> AMY

At any rate I arrived in town not ten days ago, full of dreams and
aspirations, anxious to make my way in the world . . .

Norville pours a glass of whiskey and brings it to her.

. . . a little naive perhaps but – thank you – armed with
determination, a solid work ethic, and an indomitable belief in
the future –

> NORVILLE

I myself –

He crosses back to the desk.

> AMY

Only to have that belief, that unsullied optimism, dashed against
the marble and mortar of the modern workplace –

*Norville takes a cigarette from a large wooden cigarette box on the desk
and sticks it in his mouth.*

> NORVILLE

Cigareet?

> AMY

No thank you. Seek and ye shall find, work and ye shall –

*Norville has been pushing the cigarette box towards her. It tilts lazily
forward and then disappears over the lip of the desk. We hear the thud of
the box landing on the carpet amid the pitter-patter of raining cigarettes.*

68

Amy plows on:

> . . . work and ye shall prosper – these were the watchwords of my
> education, the ethos of my tender years; these were the values
> that were instilled in me while I was growing up in a little town
> you've probably never heard of –

Norville points to the whiskey bottle.

NORVILLE

Mind if I join you?

AMY

Be my guest. A little town you've probably never heard of, a
dusty little crossroads of which you've probably never heard –

*Norville tosses back a drink and loudly gags. Eyes a-bulge, he leaps to his
feet, waves his arms and rasps as he scuttles across the room:*

NORVILLE

Excuse me – I – executive washroom . . .

He lurches through a side door.

*On his exit, Amy leaps to her feet and scurries over to his desk. At the top
of her voice:*

AMY

Are you all right?

*She flings open the top desk drawer. A lonely lead pencil rolls through the
otherwise empty drawer.*

*She expertly flips a cigarette into her mouth and strikes a match off the
desktop.*

> . . . Is it your lunch? The chicken à la king?

NORVILLE'S VOICE

No, I –

*Amy throws open another drawer, empty except for an appointment book.
As she hurriedly flips through page after blank page, an arctic wind
whistles emptiness. One page only has a notation: 11:45. Address Wilkie
Grammar School Junior Achievers Club.*

AMY
Is the à la king repeating on you?

Amy shoves the appointment book back into the drawer.

NORVILLE'S VOICE
. . . I'm fine, I . . . You were saying?

She mutters:

AMY
Values . . . watchwords . . . tender years . . .

Aloud:

– A little town you've probably never heard of . . .

She hastily stubs out her cigarette and waves her hand to disperse the smoke.

. . . Muncie, Indiana.

She scurries back across the room as we hear the washroom faucet being turned off. Amy restrikes her languid pose on the couch just as the washroom door opens.

Norville gapes, one hand pressing a dripping rag to his forehead.

NORVILLE
You're from Muncie?!

AMY
Why yes, do you know it?

Norville makes pumping motions with his fists and loud syncopated grunting noises. Amy stares.

He sings, off-key:

NORVILLE
Fight on, fight on, dear old Muncie,
Fight on – hoist the gold and blue!
You'll be tattered, torn and hurtin'
Once 'The Munce' is done with you!

Amy lamely fakes singing along, coming in louder on the last, obvious rhyme. Norville jumps an octave on it; she quickly follows suit, also pumping her fists.

As Norville crosses his hands and locks thumbs in front of his nose to make bird wings of his extended fingers –

   . . . GooooOOOO EAGLES!

– Amy awkwardly imitates.

Norville excitedly goes to his desk.

   . . . A Muncie girl! What do you know about that?! Tell you what, Amy, I'm gonna cancel the rest of my appointments this afternoon and get you a job here at the Hud!

AMY

Oh, no, really, I –

NORVILLE

Don't bother to thank me, it's the easiest thing in the world. Matter of fact, I know where a vacancy just came up.

He hits the intercom.

   . . . Mailroom.

To Amy:

   . . . This'll only take a moment.

INTERCOM

Yeah?

NORVILLE

Good afternoon to ya, this is Norville Barnes –

INTERCOM

Barnes! Where the hell have you been! And where's my voucher?!

Norville thumps at his pockets.

NORVILLE

   . . . Well, I'm not sure where I –

INTERCOM

I need that voucher! I told you a week ago it was important!

71

NORVILLE

But, look, I'm president of the company now and I –

INTERCOM

I don't care if you're *president* of the company! I need that voucher! Now!

Click – the intercom goes dead.

NORVILLE

Oh, of all the foolish . . . Well look, why don't you work in here with me? Are you familiar with the mimeograph machine?

AMY

Of course – I went to the Muncie, uh, Secretarial Polytechnic!

Norville excitedly smacks a fist into a palm.

NORVILLE

– A Muncie girl! Can you beat that!

AMY

Well I just don't know how to thank you, Mr Barnes –

NORVILLE

Please! Norville!

As he reaches to shake:

. . . It's my pleasure!

She reaches for his hand but Norville snatches it away and, winking at her, hooks thumbs in front of his nose and makes wings of his fingers.

. . . GooooOOOO EAGLES!

Amy likewise hooks her thumbs in front of her nose, makes wings, and winks back:

AMY

GooooOOOO EAGLES!

But a pull back reveals that she is now in a newspaper office, demonstrating the fight sign to Smitty, a reporter wearing a fedora with a bent-back brim.

Smitty howls with laughter.

SMITTY

. . . Once 'The Munce' . . . Holy . . .

Amy sits behind a typewriter and, as she starts typing at eighty words per minute:

AMY

And is this guy from chumpsville?! I even pulled the old mother routine –

SMITTY

Adenoids?

AMY

Lumbago.

Smitty gives a low whistle.

SMITTY

That gag's got whiskers on it!

The phone rings and Smitty reaches for it.

AMY

I'm telling you, Smitty, the board of Hudsucker is up to something –

SMITTY
(*into phone*)

Yeah.

Behind Amy an ancient man wearing an inksman's visor and sleeve garters toils at a large checkerboard surface over which he shuffles letter tiles and black spaces.

ANCIENT PUZZLER

Say, Amy, what's a six-letter word for an affliction of the hypothalmus?

AMY
(*still typing*)

– And it's a cinch – Goiter – it's a cinch this guy isn't in on it. How much time to make the Late Final?

Smitty holds the phone away from his ear.

73

SMITTY

Chief.

Still typing, Amy whistles and nods to her shoulder. Smitty tucks the phone into it as she continues typing.

AMY

Hiya Chief, just the person I wanted to apologize to . . .

Smitty checks his watch.

SMITTY

About seven minutes.

AMY
(*still typing*)

Yeah, I was all wet about your Idea Man . . . Well thanks for being so generous . . . It *is* human, and you *are* divine . . . No, he's no faker. He's the 100 percent real McCoy beware-of-imitations genuine article: the guy is a real moron –

To the Ancient Puzzler:

– as in a five-letter word for imbecile –

Back into phone:

– as pure a specimen as I've ever run across . . . Am I sure he's a nitwit? Heck, if working at the *Argus* doesn't make me an expert then my name isn't Amy Archer and I never won the Pulitzer Prize . . .

Her eyes narrow.

. . . In 1957 . . . My series on the reunited triplets . . . Well come on down here, hammerhead, and I'll show it to ya!

ANCIENT PUZZLER

Amy, what's a three-letter word for a flightless bird?

AMY

Not now, Morris, I'm busy – That's right, I said hammerhead, as in a ten-letter word for a smug, bullying, self-important newspaperman –

To Morris:

74

– Gnu –

Into phone:

– who couldn't find –

To Morris:

– that's G-N-U –

Into phone:

– couldn't find the Empire State Building with a compass, a road map and a native guide.

As she slams down the phone:

– or is it emu? And that's just the potatoes, Smitty, here comes the gravy: the chump really likes me. A Muncie girl!

Smitty chuckles.

SMITTY
Better off falling for a rattlesnake.

AMY
I'm tellin' ya, this guy's just the patsy and I'm gonna find out what for. There's a real story here, Smitty, some kind of plot, a set-up, a cabal, a – oh, and say did I tell ya?!

SMITTY
He didn't offer you money.

AMY
A sawbuck!

SMITTY
Ten smackers? Let's grab a highball!

AMY
On Norville Barnes!

She rips the page out of the typewriter, swivels to face camera, and as we track in she hollers:

. . . COPY!

ROLLING PRESSES *churn out paper after paper.*

PAPERS PILE UP *one on top of the other, very many, very quickly.*

A DELIVERY MAN *throws a baled stack of papers off the back of his truck.*

THE PAPER BALE *rolls into the foreground. A hand enters frame to snip its wires and whip off the top paper.*

A PAPER BOY *in an apron and paper-boy cap mouths 'Extra! Extra!' as he holds one of the papers aloft.*

PAN UP HIS ARM *to the newspaper and, beyond it, the towering Hudsucker Building.*

ALL OF THE ABOVE DISSOLVE WITH:

A NEWSPAPER SPINNING TOWARD THE CAMERA *and stopping full frame. Its headline, over a picture of Norville smiling, is:* IMBECILE HEADS HUDSUCKER. *The subheadline: Not a Brain in his Head.*

The newspaper is angrily slammed down to reveal that Norville has been reading the inside.

His face twisting with fury, he leans for the intercom.

                    NORVILLE
Miss Smith, can you come in please to take a letter!

He mutters to himself:

     . . . of all the cockamamie . . .

Amy bustles in holding a steno pad and pencil.

     . . . Did you happen to see the front page of today's *Manhattan Argus?*

                    AMY
Well, I . . . didn't bother to read the article. I didn't think the picture did you justice.

                    NORVILLE
The picture was fine! It's what that knuckle-headed dame wrote underneath! Of all the irresponsible . . . Amy, take this down: Dear Miss Archer. I call you 'Miss' because you seem to have

                    76

'missed' the boat completely on this one! How on earth would you know whether I'm an imbecile when you don't even have the guts to come in here and interview me man to man?! No, change 'man to man' to 'face to face'. No, change 'face to face' to 'eye to eye' and 'guts' to 'common decency'. These wild speculations about my intelligence, these preposterous inventions, would be better suited to the pages of *Amazing Tales Magazine*. If the editors of the *Manhattan Argus* see fit to publish the rantings of a disordered mind, perhaps they will see fit to publish *this* letter! But I doubt it. I most seriously doubt it. As I doubt also that you could find a home at *Amazing Tales*, a periodical which I have enjoyed for many years. Yours sincerely, et cetera, et cetera . . .

He drifts into thought.

                              AMY
Is that all, Mr Barnes?

                           NORVILLE
. . . Well *you* know me, Amy, at least better than that dame does. Do *you* think I'm an imbecile?

                              AMY
I'm sure I –

                           NORVILLE
Go on, tell the truth; I trust you and I put a lot of stock in your opinion.

                              AMY
Well, I –

                           NORVILLE
Oh sure, you're biased – you're a fellow Muncian. But would an imbecile come up with this?

He whips the cover sheet off a display pad resting on an easel to reveal a large piece of graph paper with a circle rendered on it.

Amy looks, puzzled, from the circle to Norville, who proudly beams.

. . . I designed it myself, and this is just the sweet baby that can put Hudsucker right back on top.

78

Amy's look asks for more explanation.

   . . . You know! For kids!

                    AMY
   . . . Why don't I just type this up?

                 NORVILLE
Aww, naw Amy, that won't be necessary. I shouldn't send it;
she's just doing her job, I guess.

                    AMY
Well, I don't know; maybe she does deserve it. Maybe she
should've come in to face you man to man.

                 NORVILLE
Well, she probably had a deadline . . .

                    AMY
Sure, but – she could still have gotten your side, for the record!

                 NORVILLE
Well, it's done now – what's the use of grousing about it? Forget
the letter, Amy, I just had to blow off some steam . . .

Amy gets up to leave and is heading for the door when Norville adds:

   . . . She's probably just a little confused.

This brings Amy up short.

                    AMY
   . . . Confused?

                 NORVILLE
Yeah, you know, probably one of these fast-talking career gals,
thinks she's one of the boys. Probably *is* one of the boys if you
know what I mean.

                    AMY
         (*through clenched teeth*)
I'm quite sure I don't know what you mean.

                 NORVILLE
Yeah, you know, suffers from one of these complexes they have
nowadays. Seems pretty obvious, doesn't it? She's probably very

unattractive and bitter about it.

> AMY

Oh, is *that* it!

> NORVILLE

Yeah, she probably dresses in men's clothing, swaps drinks with the guys at the local watering hole, and hobnobs with some smooth-talking heel in the newsroom named Biff or Smoocher or . . .

> AMY

Smitty.

> NORVILLE

Exactly. And I bet she's ugly. Real ugly. Otherwise why wouldn't they print her picture next to her byline?

> AMY

Maybe she puts her work ahead of her personal appearance.

> NORVILLE

I bet that's exactly what she tells herself! But you and I both know she's just a dried-up bitter old maid. Say, how about you and I grab a little dinner and a show after work? I was thinking maybe *The King and I –*

WHAP! *Amy slaps him.*

He considers.

. . . How about *Oklahoma?*

> AMY

Norville Barnes, you don't know a thing about that woman! You don't know who she really is! And only a numbskull thinks he knows things about things he knows nothing about!

As she stalks out of the office Norville stares, rubbing his cheek.

> NORVILLE

. . . Say, what gives?

A STEAM WHISTLE

Shrieking.

A TIME CLOCK

Showing five o'clock. Busy hands punch out.

EMPTY EXECUTIVE HALLWAY

A security man walks down the hall, whistling, swinging a ring of keys. After he passes the door to the ladies' room it opens and Amy peeks out, emerges, and goes to Norville's office.

NORVILLE'S OFFICE

Amy goes to the desk, takes out his appointment book, flips through it.

THE BOOK

Still empty except for the one date with the Wilkie Grammar School Junior Achievers Club, which now has a red line drawn through it and the subnotation CANCELED.

AMY

She glances around the office and – notices something.

A SMALL DOOR

It is topped by a plaque: AUTHORIZED PERSONNEL ONLY.

Amy tries the knob, which turns, and enters.

THE ROOM

It is big and dim and several stories high, with spiral staircases reaching into, and catwalks criss-crossing, the gloom above. It is filled with contraptions – works, cogs, gears. There is no window, but on what would be the window wall there is an enormous iron ring with a metal rod sweeping an interior circle. It is the back of the great Hudsucker Clock.

Amy gazes about. She crosses to a door opposite the one she entered through.

She stoops to peak through its keyhole.

AMY'S POV

We are looking into Sidney J. Mussburger's office. Mussburger sits at his desk barking into a dictaphone. Click-click-click – the perpetual-motion balls on his desk are going full-tilt; THRUMMMMmmmm – the clock's exterior second hand sweeps a shadow across the office. Mussburger, it seems, never sleeps.

MUSSBURGER

Memo. From the desk of Sidney J. Mussburger. Executive order number 530 slash A49. To: Director of the Jacksonville Facility. Copies to: Legal Affairs, Business Affairs, Central Files. Re: Movement of Raw Materials from the Huron Facility. Due to unfavorable news in the slag markets, Jacksonville inventory must be reduced by 15 percent with overflow diverted to the Waukegan Stamping Facility. Memo. From the desk of Sidney J. Mussburger. Executive order number 530 slash A50. To: Director of –

VOICE

Watchoo doin' down they, Miss Archuh?

AMY

Huh?!

She straightens and turns.

Facing her is an old black man in a janitor's jumpsuit with HUDSUCKER INDUSTRIES/The Future Is Now *stitched on it. We might recognize his voice as that of the narrator who opened the movie.*

AMY

Who are you? How did you know who I am?

MOSES

Ah speck ol' Moses knows jes about everything, leastways if it concerns Hudsuckuh.

82

AMY

But – who are you – what d'you do here?

MOSES

Ah keeps the ol' circle turning – this ol' clock needs plenty o' care. Time is money, Miss Archuh, and money – it drives that ol' global economy and keeps big Daddy Earth a-spinnin' on 'roun. Ya see, without that capital fo'mation –

AMY

Yeah yeah. Say, you won't tell anyone about me, will you?

MOSES

I don't tell no one nothin' lessen they ask. Thatches ain't ol' Moses's way.

AMY

So if you know everything about Hudsucker, tell me why the board decided to make Norville Barnes president.

MOSES

Well, that even suhprised ol' Moses at fust. I didn't think the board was that smart.

AMY

That *smart*?!

MOSES

But then I figured it out: they did it 'cause they figured young
Norville for an imbecile. Like some othuh people ah know.

AMY

Why on earth would they want a nitwit to be president?

MOSES

'Cause they's little pigglies! They's tryin' to inspire panic, make
that stock git cheap so's they can snitch it all up fo' themselves!
But Norville, he's got some tricks up his sleeve, he does . . .

He draws a circle in the air.

. . . you know, fo' kids? Yeah, he's a smart one, that Norville,
heh-heh, he's a caution. Wal, some folks is square, an' some is
hip . . .

He gives a jerk of his hips to punctuate.

. . . But I guess you don't really know him any better than that
board does, do ya, Miss Archuh?

AMY

Well, maybe I –

MOSES

An' only some kind a knucklehead thinks she knows things 'bout
things she, uh – when she don't, uh – How'd that go?

AMY
(*bristling*)

It's hardly the same –

MOSES

Why you don't even know y'own self – *you* ain't exactly the
genuine article are you, Miss Archuh?

AMY

Well in connection with my job, sometimes I have to go
undercover as it were –

84

MOSES

I don't mean that! Why you pretendin' to be such a hard ol'
sourpuss?! Ain't never gonna make you happy!

AMY
(*uncomfortably*)

I'm happy enough.

He chuckles.

MOSES

Okay, Miss Archuh.

He turns and walks away.

. . . I got gears to see to.

She calls after him:

AMY

I'm plenty happy!

She is answered only by whirring machinery.

MOSES

*Elsewhere in the great room he is hunkered down next to a catchment
which he buffs with a greasy rag. Amy's voice echoes up:*

AMY

. . . Hello?

MOSES
(*muttering to himself*)

Them po' young folks. Looks like Norville's in fo' the same kind
o' heartache ol' Warin' had. But then, she never axed me 'bout
dat . . .

As ominous music swells we:

FADE OUT

CHIEF'S OFFICE

He slams down a typescript.

CHIEF

I can't print that!

AMY

Why not? – it's all true! The board is using this poor guy!
They're depressing the stock so they can buy it cheap!

CHIEF

It's pure speculation! Why, they'd have my butt in a satchel!

SMITTY
(*chuckling*)

Ol' satchel-butt . . .

AMY

I know they're gonna buy that stock –

CHIEF

You don't know anything! Fact is they *haven't* bought it! The
stock is cheap, Archer! What're they waiting for?

AMY

I don't know . . .

SMITTY

Amy's hunches are usually pretty good, Chief.

CHIEF

You don't accuse someone of stock manipulation on a hunch, Ignatz! The readers of the *Manhattan Argus* aren't interested in sensationalism, gossip and unsupported speculation. Facts, figures, charts – those are the tools of the newspaper trade! Why it's almost as if you're trying to take the heat off this Barnes numbskull – like you've gone all soft on him!

SMITTY

Come on, Chief, that's a low blow. Archer's not gonna go gooey for a corn-fed idiot.

CHIEF

All right, I was out of line. But *you're* out of line with this stock-swindle story. Gimme some more of that Moron-from-Sheboygan stuff –

AMY

Muncie.

CHIEF

Whatever. *That's* what sells newspapers.

AMY

I've got an even hotter story – The Sap from the City Desk.

CHIEF

Watch it, Archer –

AMY

It's about a dim-witted editor who –

SMITTY

Easy, tough guy!

Amy reacts with sudden concern.

AMY

Does this suit look mannish to you?

Smitty laughs agreeably and gives her a companionable goose.

SMITTY
Yeah, sure – let's grab a highball.

She whirls and slaps him.

AMY

Back off – Smoocher!

As she storms off Smitty gawks, rubbing his cheek.

SMITTY

. . . Say, what gives?

AN ENGRAVED INVITATION

It reads:

>*Sidney J. Mussburger*
>*President Norville Barnes*
>*and the Board of Hudsucker Industries*
>*Cordially Invite You To*
>*The Annual Fancy-Dress Hudsucker Christmas Gala*
>*Music, Dancing, Refreshments (Dainties)*
>*Formal Evening Attire* de Rigeuer

The music over the invitation – 'We Wish You a Merry Christmas' – segues into the dance music of the Hudsucker Chamber Orchestra.

Dancing couples fill the screen. We glide among them to find Norville, standing stiffly between Mrs Mussburger and another woman, both dowagers of the Margaret Dumont mold – heavy-figured women with bosomy low-cut gowns and fluting falsetto voices.

DOWAGER

My husband is also a president – Sears Braithwaite of Bullard – d' you know him?

NORVILLE

I'm afraid I haven't had the, uh –

The women notice Amy chatting with an elderly gent.

MRS MUSSBURGER

Your companion is an ode!

MRS BRAITHWAITE

A lyric!

MRS MUSSBURGER

Are you betrothed?

NORVILLE

Oh, no, we uh – we just – you see Amy works in my office – runs
the mimeograph machine –

MRS BRAITHWAITE

Oh, the folly of youth!

MRS MUSSBURGER

Those green remembered hills!

MRS BRAITHWAITE

That bourne from which no traveller returns!

NORVILLE

Yes, I suppose it –

MRS MUSSBURGER

I once ran the mimeograph for Sidney. Though engaged at the
time to *quelqu-un d'autre*, my water-cooler romance became a
mad passion, an *amour fou*, a *foli adieu*.

NORVILLE

Well, he's certainly –

MRS MUSSBURGER

I'm brushing up on my French with the most charming man,
Pierre of Fifth Avenue – d'you know him?

NORVILLE

I'm afraid I –

MRS MUSSBURGER

Sidney and I are planning a trip to Paris and points continental –
aren't we, dear?

For Mussburger has entered to rest a hand on Norville's shoulder.

MUSSBURGER

Sure sure. I'm going to borrow Norville for a while if you don't mind, dear.

Well, frankly, I . . .

NORVILLE
You have a charming wife, Mr. Muss– uh, Sid.

MUSSBURGER
So they tell me. Norville, let me shepherd you through some of
the introductions here. Try not to talk too much; some of our
biggest stockholders are, uh – scratch that: say whatever you
want. Shake hands here with Sears Braithwaite, of Bullard.

BRAITHWAITE
Glad to know ya, Barnes.

MUSSBURGER
And this is Mr Zebulon Cardozo, one of Hudsucker Industries'
largest and most loyal stockholders.

*A businessman in formalwear and a ten-gallon hat turns to face Norville
but ignores his proffered hand.*

CARDOZO

What's this I hear about you bein' an embecile? What the hell is ailin' ya? A week ago my stock was worth twice what it is now! I'm considering dumping the whole shootin' match unless I see some vast improvement! Dammit, boy, it's a range war! Either you pull our wagons into a circle or I'm pullin' out of the wagon train!

Norville gives him a forced but hearty laugh of reassurance.

NORVILLE

No need for concern, sir; it's only natural in a period of transition for the more timid element to run for cover –

CARDOZO

So I'm yella, am I?!

He starts peeling off his tuxedo jacket.

. . . We'll see who's yella!

His wife, a small wiry woman, steps in as Mussburger drags Norville away.

MRS CARDOZO

Zebulon, you mind now and quit bein' sech an ol' grizzly.

As he reluctantly starts shrugging back into his jacket:

MR CARDOZO

Aww, I wasn't gonna hurt the boy, Lorelei . . .

NORVILLE

I'm sorry, Sid, I thought maybe if I showed him the long view –

Mussburger and Norville are approaching a debonaire man who holds a martini and is accompanied by an icy-looking wife.

MUSSBURGER

And this is Thorstensen Finlandsen, who heads a radical splinter group of disgruntled investors.

Norville nervously pumps Finlandsen's hand.

NORVILLE

Pleased to meet you, Mr Finlandsen. Say, it may interest you to

91

know I studied a little Finnish myself in high school – hope I'm not too rusty: *Tak sa spousa mit navelmen torsk –*

NORVILLE'S POV

Mrs Finlandsen shrieks in horror.

We pan over to Finlandsen who, in a rage, tosses his drink at Norville – into the lens – and launches a fist at us – BAM!

AN EMCEE

Grabbing the large old-fashioned microphone in front of the band:

> EMCEE
> Ladies and gentlemen, distinguished members of the Hudsucker board, I give you the king of swing, the ministerio of moonlight, the incredible, the unforgettable Mister Vic . . . Tenetta!

Vic Tenetta takes the microphone from the emcee who backs away, applauding. Tenetta wears a white dinner jacket and has jet-black hair sweeping out over his forehead in a roguishly pompadoured mat; one forelock droops and bounces across his forehead. He starts to croon.

SEVERAL BOARD MEMBERS

They are clustered in a dim corner of the room, smoking cigars. In the background, brilliantly spotlit, Vic Tenetta continues his song.

As Mussburger joins them:

> EXECUTIVE ONE
> How goes it, Sidney?

> MUSSBURGER
> Bad.

> EXECUTIVE TWO
> Good.

> MUSSBURGER
> But not bad enough.

> EXECUTIVE THREE

Too bad.

> MUSSBURGER

It could be better, it could be worse.

> ALL THREE EXECUTIVES

Hmmmmm.

> MUSSBURGER

The stock's got to drop another five points if we expect to get controlling interest. Norville tells me he's got some swell idea. Can't be good.

> EXECUTIVE ONE

Then it can't be bad!

> EXECUTIVE TWO

Couldn't be better if it couldn't be worse.

> ALL THREE EXECUTIVES

Hmmmmmm.

A NEARBY TERRACE

The party noise is faint here, Tenetta's song just filtering out.

We are on a full shot of the back of a man who stands facing the twinkling cityscape, but in an odd leaned-back posture, with one hand reaching up to his hidden face, his other hand pressed against the small of his back, like a man with a stiff neck tossing back a drink.

REVERSE

Amy, having just emerged onto the terrace, squints at him.

> AMY

. . . Norville?

He turns and we see that it is indeed Norville, holding a dripping ice pack against one eye.

. . . What happened?

NORVILLE

Oh. Nothing, really, just . . . the more timid investors are no
longer running for cover.

AMY

Let me look.

NORVILLE

Sid found me the ice pack.

AMY

Let me hold it or you'll have a real shiner.

NORVILLE

Thanks. People seem to be pretty hot over this imbecile story.

AMY

. . . I'm sorry.

NORVILLE

Oh, it isn't *your* fault, Amy. You're the one person who's been
standing by me through all this.

AMY

Norville . . . there's something I have to tell you. You see, I'm
not really a secretary.

NORVILLE

I know that, Amy.

AMY

. . . You do?

NORVILLE

I understand that you're not very skilled yet in the secretarial
arts. I'm not that skilled yet as president. Oh sure, I put up a big
front, but . . .

AMY

I believe in you, Norville – at least I believe in your . . .
intentions –

NORVILLE

Oh, I don't blame them, really. I guess I have sort of made a
mess of things. These folks have to protect their investment.

94

Most of them are very nice people –

AMY
Norville, you can't trust people here like you did in Muncie . . .

They gaze out at the city.

. . . Certain people are –

NORVILLE
Say, did ya ever go to the top of Old Man Larson's feed tower and look out over the town?

AMY
. . . Huh?

NORVILLE
You know, on Farm Route 17.

AMY
Oh yes! In Muncie!

NORVILLE
No. In Vidalia. Farm Route 17!

AMY
Uh – Yes. *Seven*teen. Yes, I – well no, I – I never really –

NORVILLE
The guys from the Varsity Squad would bring their dates up there to, uh . . . hold hands.

Memories haunt him.

. . . Course, I never made Varsity.

AMY
. . . There's a place I go now, the cutest little place near my apartment in Greenwich Village. It's called Ann's 440. It's a beatnik bar.

NORVILLE
You *don't* say.

AMY
Yes, you can get carrot juice or Italian coffee, and the people

95

there – well, none of them quite fit in. You'd love it. Why don't you come there with me – they're having a marathon poetry reading on New Year's Eve. I go every year.

NORVILLE
(*puzzled*)

Every year?

AMY

Well – *this* year – if it's good I plan to make it a tradition. I uh, my it certainly is beautiful –

She nods out at the city to avoid Norville's quizzical look.

. . . The people look like ants.

NORVILLE

Well, the Hindus say – and the beatniks also – that in the next life some of us will come back as ants. Some will be butterflies. Others will be elephants or creatures of the sea.

AMY

What a beautiful thought.

NORVILLE

What do you think you were in your previous life, Amy?

AMY

Oh, I don't know. Maybe I was just a fast-talking career gal who thought she was one of the boys.

NORVILLE

Oh no, Amy, pardon me for saying so but I find that very far-fetched.

AMY

Norville there really is something I have to tell you –

NORVILLE

That kind of person would come back as a wildebeest or a warthog. No, I think it more likely that you were a gazelle, with long graceful legs, gamboling through the underbrush. Perhaps we met once, a chance encounter in a forest glade. I must have been an antelope or an ibex. What times we must have had –

96

foraging together for sustenance, snorfling water from a
mountain stream, picking the grubs and burrs from one
another's coats. Or perhaps we simply touched horns briefly and
went our separate ways . . .

AMY

I wish it were that simple, Norville. I wish I *was* still a gazelle,
and you were an antelope or an ibex.

NORVILLE

Well, can I at least call you deer? Ha-ha-ha-ha-ha! Seriously,
Amy, the whole thing is what your beatnik friends call 'Karma' –
the great circle of life, death and rebirth.

AMY
(*morosely*)

Yeah, I think I've heard of that. What goes around comes
around.

NORVILLE

That's it. A great wheel that gives us each what we deserve.

He slaps his fist into his palm.

. . . I've gotta show Sidney and the guys that I deserve all their
confidence! Tomorrow's my big presentation to the board!

AMY
(*sadly*)

Oh, Norville –

NORVILLE

Kiss me once, Amy! Kiss me once for luck!

AMY

Sure, Norville, sure . . .

She gives him a peck. They look at each other.

. . . Oh Norville!

She embraces him. They kiss again.

Norville's eyes widen.

97

VIC TENETTA

Crooning the end of his song.

DANCING COUPLES

Turning to the bandstand to applaud.

NORVILLE AND AMY

In the middle of a passionate kiss.

FADE OUT

DOUBLE OAK DOORS

A secretary is hanging up a sign that reads: Quiet Please! Board
Meeting in Session. *From inside the boardroom we hear a muffled
whoosh-whoosh.*

INSIDE

*We are close on Norville – chest and up. His upper torso is swaying, his
shoulders rhythmically rolling as he talks. The whooshing sound is louder.*

> NORVILLE
> You know . . . for kids! It has economy, simplicity, low
> production cost and the potential for mass appeal, and all that
> spells out great profitability . . .

CLOSE ON MUSSBURGER

*Staring, holding a just-lighted but forgotten cigar in one hand and a
still-burning match in the other.*

> NORVILLE (*off*)
> . . . I had the boys down at R & D throw together this prototype
> so that our discussion here could have some focus . . .

THE BOARD

Staring, also in arrested motion, much like their reaction to Waring Hudsucker's jump.

> NORVILLE (*off*)
> . . . and to give you gentlemen of the board a first-hand look at just how exciting this gizmo is . . .

WIDER ON NORVILLE

Still gyrating, adeptly keeping the hula hoop in motion around his waist.

> NORVILLE
> . . . It's fun, it's healthy, it's good exercise; kids'll just love it, and we put a little sand inside to make the whole experience more pleasant. But the great part is we won't have to charge an arm and a leg!

Mussburger's forgotten match has burned down to his fingertips. With a wince, he shakes it out.

After a stupefied beat:

> ELDERLY EXECUTIVE
> What if you tire before it's done?

> EXECUTIVE TWO
> Does it have rules?

> EXECUTIVE THREE
> Can more than one play?

> EXECUTIVE FOUR
> (*to Executive Three*)
> What makes you think it's a game?

> EXECUTIVE THREE
> Is it a game?

> EXECUTIVE FIVE
> Will it break?

> EXECUTIVE SIX
> It better break eventually!

                    EXECUTIVE TWO
Is there an object?

                    ELDERLY EXECUTIVE
What if you tire before it's done?

                    EXECUTIVE FIVE
Does it come with batteries?

                    EXECUTIVE FOUR
We could charge extra for them.

                    EXECUTIVE SEVEN
Is it safe for toddlers?

                    EXECUTIVE THREE
How can you tell when you're finished?

                    EXECUTIVE TWO
How do you make it stop?

                    EXECUTIVE SIX
Is that a boy's model?

                    EXECUTIVE THREE
Can a parent assemble it?

                    EXECUTIVE FIVE
Is there a larger model for the obese?

                    ELDERLY EXECUTIVE
What if you tire before it's done?

                    VERY ELDERLY EXECUTIVE
What the hell is it?

                    NORVILLE
It's . . . it's . . . well, it's . . .

                    MUSSBURGER
Brilliant.

The board looks uncomprehendingly at Mussburger.

. . . It's genius. It's just exactly what Hudsucker needs at this
juncture. Sure sure, a blind man could tell you that there's an
enormous demand for this, uh . . . this uh . . .

He smiles weakly at Norville.

> . . . Congratulations, kid – you've really outdone yourself.
> Reinvented the wheel. I'm going to recommend to the board that
> we proceed immediately with this, uh . . . with the, uh . . . that
> the dingus be mass-produced with all deliberate speed. Of
> course, as president of the company the ultimate decision is
> yours.

NORVILLE

Well . . . *I'm* for it!

Furiously busy music builds to:

TELETYPE *chattering out* EXECUTIVE DIRECTIVE *#37451–JL7. A
hand enters frame to rip the directive from the teletype, then hurriedly rolls
it up and slips it into a cylindrical metal capsule.*

The capsule is popped into a pneumatic tube.

PNEUMATIC PIPING *somewhere in the labyrinthine substructure of the
Hudsucker Building. We hear a missile furiously hurtling toward us
inside the pipe.*

REVERSE *on another length of piping as we hear the capsule rocket away.*

BLINKING RED LIGHTS *on a huge board that says* HUDSUCKER
DESIGN DEPARTMENT. *Flashing red letters announce:* INCOMING
DIRECTIVE.

*The pneumatic-tube spout shoots out a cylinder and a hand eagerly yanks
it out of frame.*

A TECHNICIAN *in white laboratory smock reads the directive, nodding
soberly, as several other white-jacketed technicians crowd around to read
over his shoulder.*

A LARGE SHEET OF GRAPH PAPER *is unrolled on a drafting table.*

Under the caption TOP VIEW *is a perfect circle. Under the caption*
HORIZONTAL PROJECTION *is a horizontal line. Under the caption*
VERTICAL PROJECTION *is a vertical line.*

A hand enters frame to stamp the drawing APPROVED.

TWO MORE LENGTHS OF PNEUMATIC PIPE *as we hear another cylinder*
rocketing by.

SWISH PAN TO FROSTED DOUBLE GLASS DOORS

Lettered on the frosted glass is: ADVERTISING DEPARTMENT – *Creative*
Bullpen. Casting sharp silhouettes on the frosted glass are the three admen
working inside. Two pace back and forth, smoking cigarettes as they toss
out ideas. The third sits slumped in front of a silhouette typewriter, his head
resting on its keyboard, one hand resting on a half-empty whiskey bottle.

In the foreground, on our side of the frosted glass and so not in silhouette, a
bored secretary sits reading War and Peace, Volume I.

                    ADMAN ONE
   We'll call it the Flying Donut!

                    ADMAN TWO
   The Dancing Dingus!

                    ADMAN ONE
   The Circle o' Gaiety!

                    ADMAN TWO
   The Belly-Go-Round!

                    ADMAN ONE
   Uncle . . . Midriff!

PNEUMATIC PIPING

A cylinder rockets by.

SWISH PAN TO ACCOUNTING-DEPARTMENT WALL PLAQUE

Hanging above the accounting floor is an enormous reproduction of the
design department's rendering of the hula hoop. Over the rendering a
banner asks: WHAT WILL THIS COST?

A boom down from the poster reveals an open floor where accountants sit at rows and rows of desks. All look up at the hanging poster as they operate manual adding machines to the same beat.

The accountants wear identical vests, shirtsleeves, garters, visors and spectacles.

THE HEAD ACCOUNTANT *sits in front of the room, overseeing their efforts. He wears a full three-piece suit.*

A HUGE BOOK *is dropped onto his desk. Its cover reads:* SUMMARY OF COST ANALYSIS.

The book is opened and its pages, filled with rows of numbers, are flipped to the last page where we quickly pan down to:

THE BOTTOM LINE: *Unit cost . . .* .59
Suggested Retail 79

AN ACCOUNTANT *hovers over the Head Accountant's shoulder, waiting for his reaction.*

The Head Accountant grimly shakes his head.

BACK TO THE BOOK *as the accountant's hand enters to scratch in a 1 in front of the suggested retail of .79.*

A hand enters frame to stamp the bottom line: APPROVED.

PNEUMATIC PIPES *with more hurtling cylinders.*

THE ADVERTISING DEPARTMENT, *where the foreground secretary now reads* War and Peace, Volume 2.

> ADMAN ONE
> We need something short.

> ADMAN TWO
> Sharp.

                    ADMAN ONE
Snappy.

                    ADMAN TWO
With a little jazz.

                    ADMAN ONE
The Shazzammeter!

                    ADMAN TWO
The Hipster!

Drawing a circle in the air:

                    ADMAN ONE
The Daddy-O!

ROCKETING PIPES *forking, joining, overlapping, criss-crossing.*

THE PROVING FACILITY, *wherein men in asbestos suits scurry and dive for cover behind a bank of sandbags.*

The reverse shows a mannequin with a hula hoop fixed around its waist and dynamite strapped to its chest.

Brawny arms depress a plunger.

A fierce explosion illuminates the sandbags. As the explosion subsides:

The workmen cautiously peek out over the sandbags, then flip back their visors to watch:

The hula hoop, bouncing amid the flaming debris of the explosion, still intact.

ROCKETING PIPES

ADVERTISING DEPARTMENT

The foreground secretary now reads Anna Karenina. *The silhouetted admen, frustrated and hoarse, are still at it:*

                    ADMAN ONE
The Hoopsucker!

ADMAN TWO

The Hudswinger!

ADMAN ONE

The Hoopsucker!

ADMAN TWO

The Hudswinger!

The third adman, slouched at the typewriter, finally raises his head.

ADMAN THREE

Fellas. Fellas!

ADMAN ONE

Ya got somethin'?

ADMAN TWO

Ya got something?

ADMAN THREE

Fellas! I got somethin'!

PIECE OF ART PAPER

Printed at the top:

Hudsucker Industries Proudly Presents

Pan down to reveal:

THE HULA HOOP

Pan down to reveal:

An artist's hand working in fast motion to render the hula-hoop logo: a grinning boy with a spray of freckles, one fist thrown forward, the other drawn back, a hula hoop and its action lines spinning round his waist.

In seconds the artist has completed the logo and now, also in fast motion, he writes the slogan on either side of the boy: 'You Know . . . For Kids!'

The page is ripped off the art pad.

A GRIMY ARM *throws an enormous switch.*

MACHINES *grind into motion.*

A DONUT SPOUT *begins to spit hula hoops in massive numbers.*

A BALE OF HULA HOOPS *is loaded into a Hudsucker truck to complete its load. The truck door is slammed shut.*

AN IRON GRILL *is thrown up to reveal the display window of a toy store just opening for the day. In the window is an enormous hula hoop display, with various hoops strung up on wire in front of the finished hula hoop poster – 'You Know . . . For Kids!'*

Reflected in the display window we see people walking by, indifferent to the display. Inside the shop we see the proprietor by the cash register, his chin propped glumly in his hands.

IN NORVILLE'S OFFICE *Norville sits anxiously awaiting the verdict of Amy, who sits hunched over the ticker-tape machine, studying the emerging tape. Amy finally looks up and sadly shakes her head.*

BACK TO THE SHOP WINDOW, *where crowds still pass indifferently by. The shopkeeper stands idly in his doorway, smoking a cigarette.*

We track in on the poster. The displayed price of $1.79 has been crossed out. Inked in beneath it: Reduced: $1.59.

BACK IN NORVILLE'S OFFICE *Norville nervously paces. Amy studies the ticker tape. Once again she is forced to sadly shake her head.*

THE SHOP'S PRICE DISPLAY. *The old $1.59 is suddenly covered as a hand enters frame to slap a sticker on top of it: $1.49. A beat. The hand enters to slap on a new sticker: $1.29. Then in rapid-fire succession: $0.99. $0.79. $0.49 Two For $0.25. Free With Any Purchase.*

THE ALLEY BEHIND THE SHOP, *where garbage sits waiting for collection.*

Hands appear at the back door of the shop hurling a clutch of hoops toward the trash heap. One errant hoop rolls toward the mouth of the alley.

THE MOUTH OF THE ALLEY *as the escaped hula hoop emerges and heads off down the street.*

AN INTERSECTION *as the hoop rolls across. Cars violently brake to avoid it.*

A STREETCORNER *that the hula hoop rounds. It rolls up to a little boy, rolls in a circle around him, and finally wobbles to the pavement.*

The little boy looks at it, steps inside it, raises it to his hips, and starts hula-hooping. Somewhere a bell is ringing.

A NEARBY SCHOOLHOUSE, *its bell ringing. The front doors fly open and scores of schoolchildren run out, screaming, in a pack.*

THE STREETCORNER *as the screaming pack of schoolchildren come around and – stop short, their screams dying away.*

They stare, fascinated, at the hula-hooping youngster.

The children are dumbfounded. It is a moment of either deep mystery or deep revelation.

They start screaming.

They are running once again, maniacal, possessed. We don't know where they are running, but we might guess.

THE TOY STORE – *whose proprietor reacts as the howling pack of children sweeps in.*

BACK TO NORVILLE'S OFFICE , *where Norville sits slumped, his head resting on the desktop, utterly dejected.*

Suddenly the ticker tape burps to life and starts spitting tape. Amy looks at it with mounting excitement. Finally she looks up:

> AMY
>
> . . . Norville!

Norville raises his head. Music starts to swell.

We hold on Norville's expectant face. The music builds. We hold. The music becomes a fanfare over:

BLACK-AND-WHITE TITLE CARD

It is a newsreel logo, and a solemn-voiced announcer intones:

                        ANNOUNCER
Rockwell News presents . . . Tidbits of Time! World news in pictures, we kid you not!

Candid black-and-white film shows Norville getting out of a car, noticing the camera, grinning, and waving as he walks.

. . . As Old Man 1958 hobbles toward his finish, 'Barnes' is the name on every American lip – Norville Barnes, young president of Hudsucker Industries, a boy bred in the heartland, but now the toast of New York. Barnes is the brainy inventor of America's craziest craze, the hula hoop. Reaping untold profits for his company, the hula hoop is winning a place in the hearts – and hips! – of all American youngsters. – Whoa-ho! Did I say youngsters?! Here's Mom, taking a break from her household chores . . .

A woman switches off her vacuum cleaner, picks up a hula hoop that is conveniently leaning against a nearby wall, and starts hula-hooping.

. . . and even Dad is 'swinging' into the act!

In the office, Dad, smoking a pipe, hula hoops as well.

. . . Cards, letters, congratulations come pouring in, from Kankakee to Petaluma – including one very special long-distance call!

In jerky cinema-vérité *footage a woman is excitedly sticking her head in Norville's office door.*

                        WOMAN
He's on! He's on the line!

Swish over to Norville, agog, who picks up his phone and brings out in a breaking voice:

NORVILLE

. . . Hello?

CRACKLING VOICE

Hello, Norville. This is the President . . .

A half-wipe leaves a split screen with Norville on one side and on the other a still photo of Ike standing in a tank turret, pointing commandingly. Under the photo: VOICE OF GENERAL DWIGHT D. EISENHOWER.

NORVILLE

Oh my God, sir!

IKE

I just wanted to congratulate you. I'm very proud of you, Norville . . .

NORVILLE

Oh my God, sir!

IKE

Mrs Eisenhower is very proud of you. The American people are very proud of you.

FLASH-BULB EXPLOSION EFFECTS A CUT TO NORVILLE, *who awkwardly faces a battery of reporters.*

REPORTER ONE

Mr Barnes, how'd ya come up with the idea for the 'hula hoop'?

NORVILLE

Well, it was no great idea, really. A thing like this, it takes a whole company to put it together, and I'm just grateful for the opportunity –

REPORTER TWO

Mr Barnes, did you have any idea there'd be such a huge response?

NORVILLE

Well, frankly, I don't think anybody expected this much hoopla –

He is surprised by a burst of laughter.

> REPORTER THREE
>
> 'Hoopla on the hula hoop' – can we quote you on that, Mr Barnes?

> NORVILLE
>
> Well sure, I guess –

> REPORTER FOUR
>
> Mr Barnes, are you thinking of giving yourself a nice fat raise?

> NORVILLE
>
> Ha-ha-ha-ha. Come on, guys . . .

FLASH-BULB EXPLOSION EFFECTS A CUT BACK TO THE NEWSREEL

A scientist in a laboratory smock stiffly faces the camera. Behind him other scientists study a hoop that has been hooked up to a gyroscopic-looking device that analyzes its various movements and properties.

> ANNOUNCER
>
> What scientific principle explains the mind-bending motion of this whipping wheel of wonder?

> SCIENTIST
>
> Ze dinkus is kvite zimple, really. It operates on ze same principle zat keeps ze earth spinning round ze sun, and zat keeps you from flying off ze earth into ze coldest reaches of outer space vere you vood die like a miserable shvine! Yeees, ze principle is ze same, except for ze piece of grrrit zey put in to make ze whole experience more pleasant –

TRACK IN TO THE MEAN LAUGH

Norville, in his office, sits behind his desk in long shot. He is laughing as we begin to track in. But there is something disconcerting about his laugh – it is harder, colder, more businesslike than the dopey laugh that accompanied his elevation to the presidency. Or perhaps it is only our imagination, for, while we are still some distance away:

III

FLASH-BULB EXPLOSION EFFECTS A CUT TO ANOTHER NEWS
CONFERENCE

*Newsmen follow Norville as he walks through the lobby of the Hudsucker
Building.*

> REPORTER ONE
>
> Mr Barnes, did the board consider you an 'Idea Man' when they
> promoted you from the mailroom?

> NORVILLE
>
> Well, I guess so – I don't think they promoted me because they
> thought I was a schmoe.

> REPORTER TWO
>
> Mr Barnes, what's the next big idea for you and Hudsucker
> Industries?

> NORVILLE
>
> Jeez, I don't know. An idea like this sweet baby doesn't just
> come overnight –

> REPORTER THREE
>
> Mr Barnes, are you –

> NORVILLE
>
> – although I'll tell you one thing: I certainly didn't expect all this
> 'hoopla'!

*This tired old joke brings some polite laughter. Norville smiles as he enters
the elevator. As its doors start to close:*

> NORVILLE
>
> . . . And you can quote me on that!

FLASH-BULB EXPLOSION EFFECTS A CUT BACK TO THE NEWS-
REEL

> ANNOUNCER
>
> Yes, it's hula hula everywhere! From the cocktail parties of the
> Park Avenue smart set . . .

*A group of people in formalwear are sipping highballs and chatting as
they keep hoops in motion round their waists.*

. . . to sweethearts who want to be married in the 'swing' of things . . .

A young couple stands before the altar hula-hooping.

. . . To our friend the Negro, in the heart of the dark continent.

We pan down from an elephant to show two natives hula-hooping as they grin into the camera.

RETURN TO THE MEAN LAUGH

Yes, as we draw closer, it seems clear that Norville's laugh has grown harder, more predatory.

FLASH-BULB EXPLOSION EFFECTS A CUT TO NORVILLE *sitting in a barber chair, face lathered up, as reporters crowd in.*

REPORTER ONE
Mr Barnes, Mr Barnes, *Rumpus Magazine* has called you the most eligible bachelor of the year and the society pages have been linking you with high-fashion model Za-Za. Would you care to comment?

A burning cigar emerges from the lather around Norville's face. It waggles as he talks.

NORVILLE
There's no truth to the rumors; we're just dear friends . . .

He looks to one side.

. . . Isn't that right, Za-Za?

SWISH PAN TO ZA-ZA *standing nearby. Every man's dream, in a tarty sort of way.*

ZA-ZA
Gr-r-r-r-r-r-r-oww!

REPORTERS
Ho-leeee! Ha-cha!

Mr Barnes, whither Hudsucker? Whither Norville Barnes?

REPORTER THREE

How do you respond to the charges that you're out of ideas? Has Norville Barnes run dry?

The barber is periodically pinching Norville's nose to shave under it; as he alternately pinches and releases, Norville's voice breaks from nasal to normal and back.

NORVILLE

Not at all. Why just this week I came up with several new sweet ideas. A larger-model hula hoop for the portly. A battery option for the lazy and handicapped. A model with more sand for the hard-of-hearing. I'm earning my keep.

REPORTER FIVE

Speaking of that, Mr Barnes, do you expect to get a raise?

NORVILLE

Well by anyone's account I've saved Hudsucker Industries; our stock is worth more now than it's ever been. So, yes, I expect to be compensated for that.

END TRACK IN ON THE MEAN LAUGH

The continuing track in on Norville ends in close shot, his hands clasped on the desktop in front of him as he finishes his hard, square-jawed, man-on-top laugh, gazing flintily into the camera.

NORVILLE

– ha-ha-ha-HA-HA!

PULL BACK FROM A WEEPING EXECUTIVE

The pull back reveals that we are at a board meeting. The board members sit around the table except for Mussburger, who, a towel around his waist, is receiving a choppity-chop massage on a padded table from a muscular man in a bulging T-shirt.

MUSSBURGER

Pull yourself together, Addison.

Addison, the blubbering executive, snuffles.

ADDISON

Nobody told me! Nobody told me! You sold *all* of our stock?

MUSSBURGER

We dumped the whole load.

ADDISON

I had twenty thousand shares! I'd be a millionaire now!

MUSSBURGER

Sure sure, we'd all be millionaires. There's no point in looking
back. At the time, Stillson thought dumping our position would
panic the market, further depress the stock – then we'd buy it all
back, and more of course, once it got cheap –

ADDISON

Cheap! CHEAP! It's never been more valuable! And I'm ruined!
Ruined!

He climbs up onto the boardroom table.

. . . I'm getting off this merry-go-round!

EXECUTIVE

Addison!

ANOTHER EXECUTIVE

Myron!

ADDISON

AAAAAHHH!

*Addison runs down the length of the table and hurls himself at the
window where:*

THWOK!

*He flattens against the glass, his face squushed, his outflung hands pasted
against the window.*

All stare in horror for a long silent beat.

With the sound of a squeegee being drawn across glass, Addison, still frozen, slides down the window, hits the floor, and tips stiffly back like a felled tree.

Mussburger sits up and plants a cigar in his mouth.

> MUSSBURGER
> Plexiglass. Had it installed last week.

> ELDERLY EXECUTIVE
> . . . Myron?

> MUSSBURGER
> All right, so the kid caught a wave. So right now he and his dingus are on top. Well, this too shall pass. Myrtle J. Mussburger didn't raise her boy to go knock-kneed at the first sign of adversity. I say, we made this chump and we can break him. I say, the higher he climbs the harder he drops. I say, yes, the kid has a future, and in it I see shame, dishonor, ignominy and disgrace. Sure sure, the wheel turns, the music plays, and our spin ain't over yet.

NORVILLE'S OFFICE

A small chamber orchestra sit playing Eine Kleine Nachtmusik. *Norville, eyes closed, reclines in his desk chair, one uniformed woman stooping in front of him to manicure his nails, another, behind, massaging his temples.*

A goateed French sculptor wearing a white smock and a beret squints at Norville and chips at a block of marble with a stone-chisel and hammer.

A goon sits off to one side, hat insolently atop his head, reading the funny papers.

At length Norville stirs, opens his eyes, and sits bolt upright, batting away the hands of the manicurist and the temple-massager.

> NORVILLE
> Hold it! . . .

The musicians' playing dribbles off to silence.

. . . Nobody move, nobody breathe . . .

All sit frozen.

. . . An *idea* . . . is coming . . .

Eyes narrowed, he gazes off into space, squinting for his idea.

NORVILLE'S FINGERTIPS

which are suspended over the manicurist's soaking-bowl. A bead of water is collecting on one finger.

It drops.

THE BOWL

In slow motion the drop of water – Plooooonk! – hits.

THE MANICURIST

She flinches.

NORVILLE

One eye squints open.

NORVILLE

It's *gone* now.

The musicians resume playing. Everyone else resumes work. The intercom buzzes and a female voice announces:

INTERCOM

Miss Amy here to see you.

Norville leans forward for the intercom.

NORVILLE

Is she in the book? –

The door bursts open.

AMY

For Pete's sake, Norville!

NORVILLE

Oh! Hello, Amy – was it – I thought she said *Mamie* –

AMY

Never mind about that . . .

She shakes a piece of paper at Norville.

. . . You know what those nincompoops in the boardroom are doing?

NORVILLE

Well I wouldn't call them nincom –

AMY

They're going to discharge eight per cent of the workforce here at Hudsucker. Why, in New York alone that means eighteen hundred people out of work, people with wives and children and families –

NORVILLE

Well yes, we're pruning away some of the dead wood, but if –

AMY

You mean you *know* about this?

NORVILLE

Know about it? You think the board would do anything like this
without my authorization? No, this was my idea from the start.

AMY

Your i–

NORVILLE

We have to be realistic, Amy. You know things have slowed down
a little here at Hudsucker –

AMY

You're awful kind to yourself, Norville Barnes – the fact is *you've*
slowed down, sitting up here like a sultan not doing a lick of work!
Why, you know ideas are the lifeblood of industry and you haven't
come up with one since the hoop and the reason's plain to see!
You've forgotten what made your ideas exciting for you in the first
place – it wasn't for the fame and the wealth and the mindless
adulation of *would you get out of here*?!

*This last was addressed to the chamber orchestra, whose playing dribbles
away. They rise to pack their instruments and sheepishly leave the office.*

. . . I've been watching you, Norville Barnes, even though you've
been trying to avoid me –

NORVILLE

Now, Aim–

AMY

Shutup! – and don't think I haven't noticed how you've changed.
I used to think you were a swell guy – well, to be honest I thought
you were an imbecile –

NORVILLE

Now, Aim–

AMY

Shutup! – but then I figured out you *were* a swell guy, a little slow
maybe but a swell guy! Well, maybe you're not so slow but you're
not so swell either and it looks like you're an imbecile after –

NORVILLE

Now, Aim–

AMY

Shutup! – after all! You haven't talked to me for a week and now I'm going to say my piece. I've never been dumped by a fella before and that hurts, but what really hurts is watching you outrun your soul chasing after money and ease and the respect of a board that wouldn't give you the time of day if you . . . if you . . .

NORVILLE

Worked in a watch factory?

This brings the goon up from his funnies.

GOON

Huh-huh-huh!

AMY
(*to the goon*)

Shutup!

(*to Norville*)

Exactly! Don't you remember how you used to feel about the

hoop? You told me you were going to bring a smile to the hips of everyone in America, regardless of race, creed or color. Finally there'd be a thingamajig that would bring everyone together – even if it kept 'em apart, spatially – you know, for kids. *Your* words, Norville, not mine. I used to love Norville Barnes – yes, love him! – when he was just a swell kid with hot ideas who was in over his head. But now your head is too big to be in over!

NORVILLE

Now, Amy –

AMY

Consider this my resignation –

THWOCK – she slaps him.

The goon is on his feet.

GOON

Hey!

CRACK – Amy kicks him in the shin.

. . . Awooooo!

AMY

– effective immediately!

She strides to the door, leaving Norville rubbing his cheek and the goon hopping on one leg.

CLOSE ON A PICTURE OF AMY

We pull back to see that it is her identification photo in her HUDSUCKER PERSONNEL *file.*

A hand brings another picture of Amy into frame – this one a newspaper clipping. She stands on a podium accepting an award; standing behind her are identical middle-aged triplets. The caption: Amy Archer of the Manhattan Argus *Receives Pulitzer Prize.*

WIDER

We are in Mussburger's office. Mussburger is seated at his desk looking at the file picture and clipping; the sign-letterer/scraper leans over his shoulder.

>   MUSSBURGER
> . . . Thank you, Aloysius. This may be useful.

FADE UP TO WHITE

PERFECT WHITE

After an imageless beat a woman enters against the unblemished white background, dressed in a clinging white robe, trailing a long diaphanous scarf. She performs a flowingly sensuous dance moderne *as a saxophone plays lasciviously bending blue notes.*

After the woman dances briefly solo, Norville enters, dancing after her, pursuing her. He is wearing a coatless suit, his sleeves rolled up, his thin tie loosened.

The woman dances around him, letting her scarf trail sinuously around his body.

We hear an echoing voice:

>   VOICE
> Buddy . . . Say buddy . . .

NORVILLE

He is slumped in his desk chair, sheened with sweat, eyes closed, licking his lips.

The echoing voice grows more present:

>   VOICE
> Buddy . . . Say buddy . . . Ya busy?
>   NORVILLE
> Huh-whuh?

Norville opens his eyes and looks stuporously about. Buzz grins down at him in his little pillbox elevator cap.

BUZZ

Looks like ya nodded off there, buddy! Say, ya got a minute?

Norville clears his throat.

NORVILLE

Oh, uh . . . Buzz . . . Is it important?

BUZZ

I like to think so! It's this little idea I been working on!

He indicates an easel facing the desk.

. . . Ya see, I don't intend to be an elevator boy forever! Take a look at this sweet baby!

The easel holds an oversized sheet of graph paper. Onto it has been rendered a TOP VIEW , which is a perfect circle, and a SIDE VIEW, which is a vertical line.

Norville gazes stupidly at the circle.

. . . Ya get it, buddy? Incredibly convenient, isn't it? Ya see –

He produces a tall glass of lemonade in which a straw sits.

. . . this is how it works: it's these little ridges on the side that give it its whammy! See, ya don't have to drink like *this* anymore –

He holds his head over the glass to drink from the vertical straw.

– Now you can drink like *this* –

He bends the straw to drink at the horizontal.

. . . I call it the Buzz-Sucker, get it buddy? – After me! *Buzz*! Why, people are just dyin' for a product like this, and the great thing is we won't have to charge an arm and a –

NORVILLE

WAIT A MINUTE!

Norville slowly rises, grabs the lemonade glass, and examines it, sneering.

. . . Why, this is worthless.

124

Huh?! But buddy –

Norville yanks out the straw and crumples it.

NORVILLE

This is the most idiotic thing I've ever seen in my life!

BUZZ

Yeah, but buddy –

NORVILLE

Nobody wants a harebrained product like this! You see, Buzz, it lacks the creative spark, the unalloyed genius that made, uh . . .

He pauses to belch.

. . . say, the hula hoop such a success.

BUZZ

But buddy –

NORVILLE

And what do you mean barging in here and taking up my valuable time?! I've got a company to run here –

BUZZ

But buddy, you were –

NORVILLE

– I can't have every deadbeat on the Hudsucker payroll pestering me with their idiotic brainwaves!

BUZZ

Geez, I'm sorry buddy –

NORVILLE

An example must be made!

Buzz looks over his shoulder, then turns back to Norville.

BUZZ

Wuddya mean, buddy?

NORVILLE

FIRED! YOU'RE FIRED! IS THAT PLAIN ENOUGH

FOR YOU, BUSTER!

Buzz's jaw drops, snapping his elastic chin strap.

                        BUZZ
Awww, buddy –

                        NORVILLE
AND DON'T CALL ME BUDDY! OUT OF HERE!
OUT!

*Buzz sinks to his knees, weeping. He clutches pathetically at Norville's
pants leg.*

                        BUZZ
Aww please, sir – this job, runnin' the elevator, it's all I got!

                        NORVILLE
GET UP!

                        BUZZ
It's okay if ya don't like the Buzz-Sucker! Just lemme keep my
job, I'm prayin' to ya!

                        NORVILLE
WE DON'T CRAWL AT HUDSUCKER INDUSTRIES!
GET OUT OF MY OFFICE! LEAVE YOUR UNIFORM
IN THE LOCKER ROOM!

Buzz stumbles away, still weeping.

                        BUZZ
I'm sorry, buddy . . . I'm sorry . . .

                        NORVILLE
Buzz . . . OFF! HA-HA-HA-HA!

Norville's laughter queasily melds with Buzz's receding sobs.

MUSSBURGER

*He stands in the boardroom, back to us, gazing out the window. With the
sound of a door opening, he turns.*

The boardroom is otherwise empty except for Norville, just entering. He

*wears plaid knickers, a little cap, and a knit shirt that shows his waist
starting to bulge. A golf bag is slung over one shoulder, the clubs covered
with booties.*

NORVILLE

Sorry I'm late, Sid. That back nine at Riverdale is really
murder.

MUSSBURGER

Sure sure, it's a tough course . . .

*He starts towards Norville, tapping a manilla file down the boardroom
table as he advances.*

. . . Well thanks for coming, kid. I thought the boardroom
would be a swell place to chat undisturbed – it seems we're
having some security problems here at the Hud.

NORVILLE

Ya *don't* say.

MUSSBURGER

Mm. Ordinarily I wouldn't bother you with it, but – this is
embarrassing, kid – it seems to concern you directly.

NORVILLE

How's that, Sid?

MUSSBURGER

It's not important in itself – some elevator boy you fired came to
me claiming you'd stolen the idea for the, uh, the hoop dingus
from him.

NORVILLE

Huh?! He – no, I – he's just – maybe I was a little rough on the
boy, ya see I –

MUSSBURGER

Ah forget it, kid, you don't have to explain to me. He's a little
person. He's nothing. Fire whoever you want. No, the problem
is who you hired. A dame – a spy as it turns out. She must have
got hold of the elevator schnook, and her paper's going to town.

He is shoving the file toward Norville, who opens it.

128

. . . Sure sure, we tried to kill the story. But the *Argus* won't play ball . . .

We track in toward Norville, who stares horrified at the file.

. . . See kid, the problem the board'll have . . . you hired this woman. Kept her on, while she made a chump out of you. Serious error of judgment . . . Business is war, kid – you take no prisoners, you get no second chances. And a boner like this . . . I'm afraid when the board meets, after New Year's, your position . . . well, it looks like you're finished . . . washed up . . .

We tighten further on Norville as Mussburger circles behind him.

. . . They've got your throat pretty well slit. And when you're dead, ya stay dead. Ya don't believe me, ask Waring Hudsucker . . . Well, tough luck, kid. You came up awful fast . . . and it's a long way down.

A HEADLINE

In screaming type:

FAKE!

Next to a picture of Norville is the subhead: Idea Man a Fraud.

Beneath a picture of Buzz in his elevator operator's pillbox hat is the caption: Stole Hoop Idea from Genius Elevator Jockey Clarence 'Buzz' Gunderson.

                              AMY'S VOICE
You can't print that!

THE CHIEF

He grins wolfishly.

                                 CHIEF
We *are* printing it! She hits the streets this evening –

SWISH PAN TO

                                SMITTY
– and she's dynamite!

                                 AMY
But Al, it's the bunk! Norville showed me his design for the whatsit the day I met him! Why, Buzz couldn't have invented it – *look* at the man – he's an imbecile!

                                 CHIEF
Archer, you're a broken record. Fact is Gunderson *did* design it – apparently he's some kind of prodigy –

                                 AMY
Says who?!

                                SMITTY
You're not the only one with sources, Amy.

                                 CHIEF
Smith has a source on the Hud board – very senior, very hush-hush!

                                 AMY
Yeah, and I'll bet his initials are Sidney J. Mussburger!

SMITTY

You've lost it Aim. You've gone soft by the looks of it – soft on the dummy from Dubuque –

AMY

Muncie!

CHIEF

Whatever! It's no dig on you, Archer, but this story is hot and you're no longer on top of it. Why, it's the scoop of the century – the other papers won't have the Gunderson dope till tomorrow – the *Allgemeinischer Zeitung, Le Figaro*, they'll be choking on our dust come mornin'.

AMY

You're fools, both of you! You're being used! Don't you see, Al –

CHIEF
(*gently*)

Amy – take a break. You've worked hard on this story – heck, you broke it for us! But it's passed you by and Smith here has taken up the slack.

AMY

You want slack, I'll give you slack. You're not putting me out to pasture, Al, I quit! Consider this my resignation –

She turns to Smitty –

– effective immediately!

– and swings – but he catches her before contact, holds her by the wrist, and sneers:

SMITTY

. . . Soft.

Amy swings her free arm to – THWACK – blindside his other cheek.

NORVILLE

In flickering black-and-white, he is lying on a couch that has been brought into his office, gazing listlessly at a bend straw, being questioned

132

by someone offscreen. The footage is rough, taking a moment to find focus; the sound is tinny.

> VOICE
> Dell me vat is first zing droppensie head ven I menzhen ze vord . . . Zex?

> NORVILLE
> (*listlessly*)
> Aww, what's the difference.

BOARD MEMBERS

Sitting in a darkened boardroom, gazing off at a screen that sends light flickering onto their faces.

> VOICE
> Und ven I zpeak of Authority?

> NORVILLE'S VOICE
> Awww, I dunno.

BACK TO THE SCREEN

> VOICE
> Eggzplain please ze zignifikanz of ze straw.

> NORVILLE
> Nuthin' really.

A shadow is thrown across the screen as a figure steps into the projector beam. He throws the sharp silhouette of a strict Freudian analyst: Vandyke beard, pince-nez with chain trailing down to his vest, one thumb hooked into the vest, the other hand holding a cigar wreathing smoke, which he waves for emphasis.

> ANALYST
> Patient dizplayed liztlessness, apathy, gloomy indifference und vas blue und mopey . . .

The image on the screen cuts to four inkblots in succession. The analyst sweeps in a pointer and thwoks each image as he comments upon it.

. . . Ven asked vut four Rorschach stains reprezented, Patient replied, 'Nussink much,' 'I don't know,' 'chust a blotch,' und 'sure beats me.'

The screen now shows a close shot of Norville on the couch, mouth listlessly agape.

. . . Patient shows no ambition, no get-up-und-go, no vim. He is riding ze grand loopen-ze-loop –

The screen image cuts to a sine wave on a graph, the top of which is labeled 'Euphoria'; the bottom, 'Despair'; and a reference line through the middle, 'Normal'. There is an X on the declining side of the wave, near the bottom, labeled 'Patient'.

– zat goes from ze peak of delusional GAIETY to ze trrrroff of dezBAIR. Patient is now near – but not yet at! – ze lowest point; ven he reachensies bottom he may errrRRUPT und pose danger to himself und uzzers.

MUSSBURGER

Casually puffing a cigar.

MUSSBURGER

Diagnosis, Dr Bromfenbrenner?

ANALYST

Patient is eine manic-depressive paranoid type B, mit acute schizoid tendencies.

MUSSBURGER

So Patient is . . . ?

He interrogatively twirls a finger round his temple.

ANALYST

Prezizely. Knots.

The board murmurs.

MUSSBURGER

Prescription?

ANALYST

SREE SINKS! Kommitment. Electro-confulsif therapy.
Maintenance in eine zecure wazilities.

*As he scores each point it is illustrated on the screen behind him: a patient
is forced into a straitjacket by two brawny, unshaven attendants; current
arcs between two leads wielded by a nurse with a starched cap and an
authoritarian bosom; and, lastly, a steel-barred door is slammed shut
behind a stooped and broken patient who is led, shuffling, away.*

Here the film runs out, chattering, and the screen goes white.

The projector is shut off and the lights go on.

The board politely applauds.

CLOSE ON A BARMAN

*He has a goatee and wears a cut-off sweatshirt, dungarees and dark
glasses, and has a phone wedged into his shoulder.*

BARMAN

Yeah, just get down here – he says he's a friend of yours . . . He
won't say, but, man, is he from Squaresville!

*He hangs up and we hinge with him to bring the length of the bar into
view. Norville, disheveled, is on the other side bellowing.*

NORVILLE

I want a martini! It's New Year's Eve and I deserve a martini!

BARMAN

Daddy, it's like I been tellin' ya –

NORVILLE

I thought you served misfits here!

BARMAN

Yeah daddy, that's a roger, but we don't sell alcohol.

NORVILLE

What kind of bar is it if ya can't get a martini?!

BARMAN

It's a juice and coffee bar, man, like I been tellin' ya –

135

NORVILLE

I want a martini! Right here, right now! I've had a martini in every bar on the way down here, and I'm not about to –

BARMAN

Martinis are for squares, man.

NORVILLE
(*suddenly enraged*)

What'd you call me?!

He starts awkwardly peeling off his suit coat.

. . . You son of a –

AMY'S VOICE

Norville!

NORVILLE

Huh?!

He looks stupidly about, the shoulders of his coat down around his elbows. As Amy rushes up:

. . . Oh, it's you! Lookin' for a nitwit to buy your lunch?!

AMY

Oh Norville, I –

Norville's attention has already left her; he is looking for the bartender.

NORVILLE

Barman! I'd like a, uh . . . martini!

AMY

Norville, I'm sorry, I . . . I tried to tell you . . . so many times . . . It's hard to admit when you've been wrong. If you could just . . . find it in your heart to – to give me another chance –

NORVILLE

Ha! Ya take no prisoners, ya get no second chances! Barfella! Set'm up!

AMY

Please Norville, please give me one more chance! And yourself too – we both deserve one! Just give us a second chance and we

136

can fight this thing! I know this last story was a lie! You've got to release a statement! I can help you write it! Brandishing this story as —

NORVILLE

Aww, what's the difference. I'm all washed up. Extinct. *Homo sapiens sappicus.*

AMY

Well, that just about does it! I've seen Norville Barnes the young man in a big hurry, and I've seen Norville Barnes the self-important heel – but I've never seen Norville Barnes the quitter, and I don't like it!

She slowly pumps her arms, chanting:

. . . Fight on, fight on, dear old Muncie . . .

She steps back off the stool. Norville watches her dully, his head swaying.

. . . Fight on – hoist the gold and blue;
You'll be tattered, torn and hurtin'
Once 'The Munce' is done with you!
GooooOOOO EAGLES!

She looks hopefully for some effect, but after staring at her for a slack-jawed beat Norville can only bring out:

NORVILLE

You lied to me! I can't believe you lied to me! A *Muncie* girl!

He lurches off his stool toward the door. Watching him, despair fights with confusion on Amy's face.

AMY

But Norville . . . I . . .

She realizes that, though shattered, he is still the simple innocent she loved –

. . . Oh, Norville!

– and bursts into tears.

Norville is staggering drunkenly up the spiral staircase.

NORVILLE

When you're dead ya stay dead – just ask Waring Hudsucker!

THE BAR EXTERIOR

It is night, snowing.

We pan to follow Norville as he lurches out of the bar, but the pan brings a newspaper into frame in close shot:

Above a picture of Norville is the headline: MUNCIE MENTAL CASE. *The subhead: Hud Chief to Tend Daisies. Sub-subhead: Headshrinker Calls Him Walking Time Bomb.*

NEWSIE'S VOICE

Extra! Extra! New Year's Eve Edition!

Norville's hand enters frame to push the newspaper away, which leaves us looking up the empty street. Norville's back enters as he stumbles away, pulling up his coat collar as he recedes, the newsie's voice continuing:

. . . Barnes' Brain Caught Red-Handed! Ideas Ersatz! Man from Muncie a Moron After All! Read all about it!

CLOSE ON NORVILLE TRUDGING

Voices well up, echoing. A face looms with each voice, floating through the limbo that surrounds the walking Norville:

VOICES

. . . You're not so slow but you're not so swell either and it looks like you're an imbecile after all . . . Noooo, I don't guess you *will* be here long . . . Sure sure, but even there they called you dope . . . dipstick . . . lamebrain . . . schmoe . . . And is this sap from chumpsville?! . . . imbecile after all . . . Tough luck, kid – you came up fast, and it's a long way down . . . Norville, you let me down . . . You let Mrs Eisenhower down . . . You let the American people down . . . It's a long way down . . . imbecile after all . . . But what really hurts is watching you lose your soul . . . Please, buddy! Runnin' the elevator – it's all I got! . . . Long way down . . . When you're dead, ya stay dead . . . Sure sure, the kid's screwy – it's official . . .

This last voice and superimposed face is Mussburger's. Norville dissolves away to leave us on Mussburger in the:

BOARDROOM

Hellishly bottom-lit board members sit around the table wearing conical New Year's hats. Mussburger, the only one not wearing a hat, waves his cigar as he continues to gloat:

> MUSSBURGER
> . . . The barred-window boys are out looking for him now, and we'll see how Wall Street likes the news that the president of Hudsucker Industries is headed for the booby hatch. Why, when Doc Bromfenbrenner gets through with him he'll need diapers and a dribble cup . . .

The board murmurs appreciatively.

> . . . Let me remind you, gentlemen, that our secret post-New Year's party will be held in the office of the president shortly after midnight tonight. Remember, it's strictly stag, so leave the wives at home; we'll be showing some films and, yes gentlemen, there *will* be exotic dancers.

Louder murmuring. One board member leers, a trace of spittle at the corner of his mouth.

> Well, if that's all . . .

HIGH, NIGHTMARISH DUTCH ANGLE

Looking down on the boardroom table.

> ALL
> # LONG LIVE THE HUD!

NORVILLE

He trudges on, faster, sweatier.

VOICES

Ring out the old! Ring in the new! . . .

People come and go, laughing, talking, blowing noisemakers, making merry.

. . . RING OUT THE OLD! RING IN THE NEW! RING OUT THE –

THOOMP *! Norville has run into someone. He looks up, dazed.*

VOICE

Say, watch where you're – Hiya, buddy!

It is Buzz, the elevator boy, dressed in an ill-fitting tuxedo and a conical party hat. Za-Za is on his arm, towering over him, sneering at Norville.

NORVILLE

Buzz!

BUZZ

Out on the town, huh? Guess what buddy! Mr Muss– . . . uh, *Sid* said I could have my old job back. I deserve a second chance he says!

NORVILLE

. . . He did?

BUZZ

Yeah, turns out old bucketbutt isn't such a bad guy after all!

NORVILLE

Gee Buzz, that's wonderf–

BUZZ

But he told me you stole that swell hoop idea from me. What gives!

NORVILLE

But Buzz –

BUZZ
(*getting angry*)

Say, that was a swell idea!

140

But Buzz, *you* know I never –

BUZZ

And Sid says you stole it!

NORVILLE

But Buzz –

ZA-ZA

Well wuddya waiting for, Clarence? – Pop him one!

BOFFO! *Buzz swings and Norville hits the snow hard.*

BUZZ

Think about *that*, Idea Man!

Norville groggily raises his head.

PASSER-BY

Say, isn't he that lunatic?

Norville looks dopily up at the swells in party hats who are starting to gather.

VOICES

. . . that big-shot faker . . . the Wall Street fraud guy . . . nuttier than a fruitcake . . . they say he's a menace . . . wuddya waitin' for, call a cop! . . .

Norville staggers to his feet. The crowd cringes.

. . . He's on his feet . . . We can take him!

Norville bursts through the crowd.

Buzz gives chase, followed by the braver souls, followed by the rest of the mob.

Norville runs, gasping, around a corner.

. . . Down here! He went down here!

Behind Norville the crowd rounds the corner, led by Buzz.

A van screeches to a halt and out jump two burly men in white, one of them holding open a straitjacket, the other carrying a large butterfly net.

They join in the chase.

Norville turns down an alley. A drunk drooping off a lamppost gaily waves a bottle.

> DRUNK
> Ring out the old! Ring in the new!

The crowd is running past the mouth of the alley, having missed Norville's turnoff.

LIMESTONE FLOOR

Norville, gasping, crashes down into frame, his hands breaking his fall against the limestone. The camera spins ninety degrees to reveal that it is not floor but wall that he has run into and is now leaning against. Norville looks up, sweating.

NORVILLE'S POV

The massive Hudsucker Building looms dizzily up, capped by the huge Hudsucker Clock.

> DISTANT VOICES
> Ring out the old! Ring in the New!

HUDSUCKER LOBBY

Norville staggers in.

A gust of icy air comes in with him and whisks a dropcloth off a huge shape that dominates the lobby:

It is the heroic statue of Norville that we earlier saw him sitting for.

Norville reels over to it, staring dumbly.

THE STATUE

Mutely – mockingly – dignified.

NORVILLE

He staggers off to the elevators.

MUSSBURGER'S OFFICE

We track across his office toward Mussburger who, feet up on his desk, cigar in one hand, laughs demonically. Click-click-click – the perpetual-motion balls swing on his desk; THRUMMmmm – the sweep second hand of the clock, illuminated now, casts moving shadows that roll across the floor. Evil prevails.

A piece of paper and a pencil lie on his desk. As we approach we pan down and swing around to read what is handwritten on the paper:

Musssucker Industries

Hudburger Industries

Sidsucker Industries.

This last alternative has been circled in red. Below it has been scribbled:

Sidney J. Mussburger, President.

Evil laughter.

Sweeping shadows.

NORVILLE'S OFFICE DOOR

Aloysius, the sign-painter, is stooped before the door, painting, as we track in. Hearing something, he looks back over his shoulder and in doing so reveals that, under 'President', Norville's name has been scraped away. Being painted in its place is SIDNEY J. MUSSBUR . . .

NORVILLE

He has just come out of the elevator. He stares, then pushes past the sign-painter.

NORVILLE'S OFFICE

Dark and empty. Norville turns on the overhead light. He peels off his coat as he staggers over to the closet.

Norville pulls his old mailroom apron from the closet and puts it on: HUDSUCKER MAILROOM /The Future Is Now.

He throws open the window.

Wind whistles.

He climbs out.

THE LEDGE

Norville, pressed back against the wall, looks cautiously down.

We hear distant chanting:

> VOICES

> Ten . . . nine . . .

NORVILLE'S POV

A sickening drop. Receding snowflakes. On the street far, far below, a lone car's headlights cut through the falling snow.

> VOICES

> Eight . . . seven . . .

WIDER ON NORVILLE

We are floating in; it is the shot with which the movie began. The sweep second hand of the Hudsucker Clock is approaching the 12 of midnight, the New Year. In sync with the clock, the chanting continues:

> VOICES

> Six . . . five . . .

We have come in close on Norville. We faintly hear a door opening inside his office. Norville looks to the side.

NORVILLE'S POV

After a beat the lit office windows go dark.

NORVILLE

He starts to shuffle back toward the open window.

                      VOICES

Four . . . three . . .

NORVILLE'S POV

An arm reaches out the open window and . . . pulls it shut.

                    NORVILLE

Hey . . .

                    VOICES

Two . . .

NORVILLE

Near the window now.

                    VOICES

One . . .

                    NORVILLE

Hey . . .

He starts to turn, crossing one leg over the other to face against the building –

BONG! The Hudsucker Clock, just nearby, is painfully loud.

Norville, startled, seems to be losing his balance in finishing his turn as we whisk off him to:

THE CLOCK

BONG! Midnight's second toll.

                    VOICES

Happy New Year!

                    NORVILLE

– No, please!

NORVILLE

He is hanging onto the icy ledge by his fingertips. His feet dangle away. Snow falls.

NORVILLE

Hey! . . .

NORVILLE'S POV

Looking steeply up. Gazing down at us through the closed window is Aloysius. His expressionless exhale momentarily steams the glass. He turns away.

BONG!

Norville struggles to keep his grip.

His fingertips slide – slide –

NORVILLE

No . . .

His fingertips slip from the edge. Empty wind.

BONG!

Norville falls silently down the facade of the Hudsucker Building.

BONG !

MUSSBURGER *is laughing.*

THE CLOCK; *its second hand making its descent.*

NORVILLE *falling.*

MUSSBURGER *laughing.*

SECOND HAND *descending.*

NORVILLE *falling – and suddenly, with a great moaning sound – he stops, suspended in mid-air, head down, feet in the air.*

He waves his arms, to no effect, and looks around.

PEOPLE IN THE STREET

Frozen in attitudes of laughter, celebration.

Snow sifts silently down around their motionless bodies.

NORVILLE

He alone can move, but doesn't fall. He looks awkwardly about, his body in a dive-bomber attitude, canted steeply down.

THE HUDSUCKER CLOCK

Its second hand is arrested on its downward sweep. Whining noises emanate from within the clock.

A GREAT GEAR

A broom handle has been jammed between two meshing cogs, stopping them. We pull back along the handle to reveal Moses, who has thrust it there, and who now turns back over his shoulder to address the camera.

MOSES
Strictly speakin' I'm never s'pose to do this, but . . . have you got a better idea?

NORVILLE

He twists back to look up over his shoulder, reacting to distant – very distant – singing.

NORVILLE'S POV

Looking up the length of the Hudsucker Building. Someone – or something – cloaked in white is descending from the stars.

148

We can make out a male voice, accompanied by strumming:

VOICE
She'll be ridin' six white horses when she comes,
She'll be ridin' six white horses when she comes . . .

MUSSBURGER'S OFFICE

Mussburger sits frozen with a gate-mouthed grin pasted to his face. On his desk the perpetual-motion balls are frozen with one ball swung out but suspended, hanging at the apex of its arc.

Through the window behind Mussburger we see a white form descending outside through the snow. Its singing is muffled by the glass.

BACK TO NORVILLE

He gapes.

THE ANGEL

– for it is an angel – arrives. He is a balding man wearing rimless glasses and a loose white robe. Large feathery wings sprout from his back and beat heavily until he comes to rest in mid-air.

He puts aside his musical instrument, a white ukelele with gold tuning heads.

ANGEL
Love that tune. How ya doin', kid?

NORVILLE
Mr . . . Mr Hudsucker?

HUDSUCKER
Ta-daaaa!

Presenting himself, he spreads his arms and stamps his forward foot, forgetting that there is nothing beneath his foot to stamp. He lurches forward, momentarily losing his balance.

. . . WOOooo!

He rights himself. The halo spinning lazily over his head has been jarred askew. With a flick of his forefinger he rights it.

. . . How d'ya like this thing? They're all wearin' 'em upstairs.

He blows a dismissive raspberry.

. . . It's a fad.

He pats at his robe, produces a white cigar.

. . . Anyway. I see you've been having, uh . . .

He casually flicks his thumb out of his fist, igniting the thumb tip. He lights the cigar off his thumb.

. . . been having some problems with the board. Now this is exactly the kind of thing IyayayeeEEEE . . .

Pain reminds him that he has forgotten to extinguish his flaming thumb, which he now waves frantically about.

. . . Jesus Christopher – That smarts . . . Where was I? Oh yeah, the board. I guess Sidney's been puttin' the screws to ya, huh Norman?

NORVILLE
Norville.

HUDSUCKER
Mm. Well, say what you like about the man's ethics, he's a balls-to-the-wall businessman. Beat ya any way he can. Straight for the jugular. Very effective.

NORVILLE
Yes sir.

HUDSUCKER
Any particular reason you didn't give him my Blue Letter?

NORVILLE
Huh?

HUDSUCKER
Jesus, Norman, just a dying man's last words and wishes, no big deal.

NORVILLE

Oh, geez, Mr Hudsucker, I apologize, there was an awful lot of excitement and I guess I must've mislaid –

HUDSUCKER

It's sittin' in your apron pocket, right where you left it. Imbecile.

Norville reaches in and – pulls out the wrinkled Blue Letter.

NORVILLE

Oh. Geez.

HUDSUCKER

Failure to deliver a Blue Letter is grounds for dismissal.

NORVILLE

Geez, I –

HUDSUCKER

Ah, it's New Year's, I'm not gonna add to your woes. I'm just saying.

NORVILLE

Yes sir.

HUDSUCKER

Anyway. You wanna read it?

NORVILLE

Sir?

HUDSUCKER

Yeah, go ahead. Might learn something. Might keep you from jumpin' outa anymore windows.

THE CLOCK ROOM

BANG – *its door is kicked open by Aloysius.*

We track in on Aloysius as he looks right, looks left, and spots:

MOSES

Whom we also track in on, standing in front of the gear groaning against his broom handle. His eyes widen.

MOSES

My word.

BACK TO NORVILLE AND HUDSUCKER

As Norville unfolds the letter and reads:

NORVILLE

. . . From the desk of Waring Hudsucker. To: Sidney J. Mussburger. Regarding: My demise. Dear Sid. By the time you read this, I will have joined the organization upstairs – an exciting new beginning. I will retain fond memories of the many years you and I –

HUDSUCKER

Yeah yeah, standard resignation boilerplate – go down to the second paragraph.

CLOCK ROOM

The whining of frustrated gears is louder, more urgent.

Moses and Aloysius circle each other, trading cautious, elderly punches. Most of them miss.

Aloysius feints left, rears back, and throws an empty right, catching air. Moses connects with a left sending Aloysius staggering back.

Aloysius pulls out his razor-scraper and advances menacingly.

BACK TO NORVILLE AND HUDSUCKER

As Norville flips a page and reads:

NORVILLE

You will no doubt be wondering why I have decided to end my tenure, both at Hudsucker and here on earth. Why now, now when things are going so well? Granted, from the standpoint of our balance sheet and financials, sure sure, we're doing fine. But in my personal life, Sidney, I have made grave errors. I have let my success become my identity, I have foolishly played the great man, and have watched my life become more and more empty as a result. My vanity drove away she who could have saved me. Oh, yes, I loved a woman once, Sid, as you well know – a beautiful, vibrant lady, an angel who in her wisdom saw fit to choose you instead of I. I –

Norville is interrupted by loud blubbering. He looks up.

Hudsucker is weeping loudly into a white handkerchief. He saws at his nose, gives it a loud honk, and urgently quavers in a voice strangled with emotion:

HUDSUCKER

Skip this part . . .

He waves his hankie in get-on-with-it circles.

. . . Next page, next page.

CLOCK ROOM

Aloysius is advancing, whooshing the razor through the air in menacing arcs, backing Moses toward the arrested gear.

BACK TO NORVILLE AND HUDSUCKER

As Norville reads, Hudsucker casually examines his fingernails, then pats down a yawn.

NORVILLE

How often, Sidney, has each of us yearned for such a second chance – in business or in love? Yes, a second chance – this brings me to our company, Sid, and its future. Our next president must have the liberty I have had, as owner, to experiment, and even fail, without fear of the whims of stockholders or an impatient board. The new president must be free to fail – and learn; to fall – and rise again, by applying what he has learned. Such is business. Such is life. Accordingly, I hereby bequeath all of my shares in Hudsucker Industries to

153

whomever you and the board shall elect to succeed me as president. I assume this will be you, Sidney. If not – if the board should choose someone else to be the new president – then –

HUDSUCKER

– tough titty toenails!

He roars with laughter.

. . . That'll show the bastard!

More laughter. Finally:

. . . Okay, go ahead.

THE CLOCK ROOM

Moses has backed up as far as he can go. Aloysius feints with the razor and connects with a left, doubling Moses back over the railing. He pounces, pinning Moses and slashing down with the razor.

Moses grabs his wrist just in time.

BACK TO NORVILLE

NORVILLE

. . . then I urge you to work with the new president, and to remind him, when he needs to be reminded, that failure should never lead to despair. For despair looks only to the past. The future is now, and when our future president needs it, Waring Hudsucker hereby bequeaths him – his second chance . . . Long live the Hud . . . Waring Hudsucker. Geez.

HUDSUCKER
(*pleased with himself*)

Yup. It's all there.

CLOCK ROOM

Moses is still pinned with one hand wrapped around Aloysius's wrist.

He throws a left-handed punch that sends Aloysius staggering back.

Moses reaches for the nearest weapon at hand – the broom – and swings it at Aloysius.

Aloysius defensively throws up his hands – grabs the broom – stumbles back against the railing.

He loses his balance and keeps going backward, over the railing, carrying the broom with him into oblivion.

ALOYSIUS

AAAAAaaaaaa . . .

The great gear is groaning into action.

As the great clock BONGS, *Moses looks down in horror at his own empty hands.*

THE HUDSUCKER CLOCK SECOND HAND

Lurching to life.

MUSSBURGER'S OFFICE

The frozen ball bearing swings down into action.

NORVILLE

After the shortest frozen beat, he plummets out of frame.

TRAVELING WITH NORVILLE

He zips down the building with what seems to be extra velocity, making up for lost time.

NORVILLE'S POV

The street spins crazily up.

NORVILLE

Covers his eyes with his hands, which still clutch the Blue Letter.

SIDE ANGLE

On the sidewalk as plummeting Norville enters face-down and – stops.

He spreads his fingers and peeks at the sidewalk an inch away.

Hudsucker distantly calls:

> **HUDSUCKER**
> Deliver that letter in the morning!

CLOCK ROOM

Moses has one hand jammed into the great gear. He pulls it out and waves it in agony.

> **MOSES**
> YAAAAAAAAA!

NORVILLE

collapses onto the sidewalk with one last mighty BONG *of the Hudsucker Clock.*

THE STREET

As people reanimate, Norville gets to his feet and dashes off into the background, frantically waving the Blue Letter.

> **NORVILLE**
> YAAAAAAAAA!

BOOM DOWN

From a tavern sign that says ANN'S 440, *to the front door, which Norville is entering.*

INSIDE ANN'S 440

Amy sits halfway down the bar, staring morosely into a coffee cup. We are pulling back.

Norville enters, sees her, and struggles through the crowd to reach her. As she looks up, Norville makes the Go Eagles sign, hooking his thumbs in front of his nose and spreading his fingers.

Two familiar voices narrate the scene, sounding tipsy:

> LOU
>
> What the heck's he doin', Benny?

Amy looks at Norville, startled. After a moment she returns the sign.

> BENNY
>
> What the heck's *she* doin', Lou?

> LOU
>
> What the heck they doin'?

Norville and Amy embrace.

> BENNY
>
> You know what they're doin' now, Lou.

> LOU
>
> This I know, Benny.

> BENNY
>
> This you're familia' with.

Norville and Amy kiss.

> LOU
>
> . . . Geez.

> BENNY
>
> . . . Geez.

We hear labored, raspy breathing.

> LOU
>
> . . . Y'all right, Benny?

In a quavering voice:

> BENNY
>
> . . . Yeah, I'm . . . it's just . . . It's beautiful, Lou!

> LOU
>
> It *is* beautiful, Benny.

Both men sound near tears as Norville and Amy continue their embrace:

> BENNY
>
> It's the most beautiful t'ing I ever saw.

> LOU
>
> . . . It's the most beautiful t'ing *I* ever saw.

Our pull back ends as the familiar beatnik bartender enters to block our view of Norville and Amy. He squints down at Benny and Lou.

> BARTENDER
>
> You cats comin' from a party?

> BENNY
>
> Cabbies' affair.

> LOU
>
> Hacks' New Year's gala.

> BARTENDER
>
> Crazy. Get you anything else? Sangria? Carrot juice? Herbal tea?

REVERSE

Benny and Lou sit side by side at the bar. Lou wears a cottony white beard and white eyebrows and a long flowing robe, and holds a cardboard scythe. An hourglass rests on the bar next to him. A sash across his robe says '1958'.

> LOU
>
> Bromo.

Benny wears an oversize diaper, a baby bonnett, and a sash across his hairy chest and thick belly that says '1959'.

He chucks himself in the heart, cocks his head and sucks in air.

> BENNY
>
> . . . Bromo.

THE BLUE LETTER

It lies open on the boardroom table. A cigar has been left smoking in an ashtray next to it, and next to that is a ticking wristwatch.

We hear the voice of Moses, the old maintenance man:

MOSES

And so began 1959. The new year . . .

We tilt up to show the length of the boardroom table and the window at its end, against which are crowded all of the board members, peering out to one side.

. . . and the start of a new business cycle. When he learned that Norville owned the comp'ny, ol' Sidney was upset at first . . .

THE OUTSIDE LEDGE

Mussburger stands nervously on the windblown ledge, cautiously dipping one toe into the void, trying to summon his nerve.

. . . It's a good thing Doc Bromfenbrenner was there . . .

We pan over to reveal that further down the ledge two men in white are inching toward Mussburger, one clutching a butterfly net, the other a straitjacket.

. . . 'cause he was able to keep Sidney from harmin' his ol' self. An' he prescribed a long rest in a sanita– . . . uh, a sanitory– . . . uh – . . . in the booby hatch.

We cut to a barred door being slammed behind a straightjacketed Mussburger, who, puffing on a cigar, is being led away.

. . . Now Norville, he went on an' ruled with wisdom and compassion . . .

BOARDROOM

Norville is enthusiastically presenting a design he has up on an easel. Under the heading BRAND NEW *is a large circle. The side view is a flat line.*

. . . and started dreamin' up them excitin' new ideas again. You know . . . for kids!

The board members look at the design, puzzled.

Norville yanks a dropcloth off of a piece of plastic on a pedestal. He has the board's complete attention.

> . . . An' that's the story of how Norville Barnes climbed away up to the forty-fourth floor of the Hudsucker Buildin' . . .

Norville picks up the plastic disc and as he sails it we cut:

OUTSIDE

The frisbee floats out the boardroom window.

MOSES
> . . . an' then fell all the way down, but didn't quite squish hisself.

We boom up, away from the boardroom, to the great Hudsucker Clock.

> . . . Ya know, they say there *was* a man who jumped from the forty-*fifth* floor . . . but that's another story. Heh-heh-heh! Ya-heh-heh-heh!

We fade out on the clock as Moses's laughter recedes and end music swells.